GOD the what?

Also Available from SkyLight Paths

Who Is My God? 2nd Edition
An Innovative Guide to Finding Your Spiritual Identity
By the Editors at SkyLight Paths

GOD the what?

What Our Metaphors for God Reveal about Our Beliefs in God

CAROLYN JANE BOHLER

Walking Together, Finding the Way®
SKYLIGHT PATHS®
PUBLISHING
Woodstock, Vermont

God the What? *What Our Metaphors for God Reveal about Our Beliefs in God*

2015 Quality Paperback Edition, Second Printing

Library of Congress Cataloging-in-Publication Data
Bohler, Carolyn Stahl, 1948–
God the what? : what our metaphors for God reveal about our beliefs in God / Carolyn Jane Bohler. —Quality paperback ed.
p. cm.
Includes bibliographical references (p.) and indexes.
ISBN-13: 978-1-59473-251-5 (quality pbk.)
ISBN-10: 1-59473-251-5 (quality pbk.)
1. God (Christianity) 2. Metaphor—Religious aspects—Christianity. I. Title.
BT103.B64 2008
231—dc22
2008032588

ISBN 978-1-59473-338-3 (eBook)

10 9 8 7 6 5 4 3 2

Manufactured in the United States of America
Cover design: Jenny Buono

SkyLight Paths Publishing is creating a place where people of different spiritual traditions come together for challenge and inspiration, a place where we can help each other understand the mystery that lies at the heart of our existence.

SkyLight Paths sees both believers and seekers as a community that increasingly transcends traditional boundaries of religion and denomination—people wanting to learn from each other, *walking together, finding the way.*

Walking Together, Finding the Way®
Published by SkyLight Paths Publishing
A Division of Longhill Partners, Inc.
Sunset Farm Offices, Route 4, P.O. Box 237
Woodstock, VT 05091
Tel: (802) 457-4000 Fax: (802) 457-4004
www.skylightpaths.com

For John,

who modeled for our own children

and the teens in his religious education classes

an unswerving commitment to naming God

in ways that are liberating for all.

CONTENTS

ACKNOWLEDGMENTS

Marcia Broucek has a good memory. We encountered each other when I was first beginning my exploration of metaphors for God. She had the insight and audacity to find me years later to inquire how my quest was proceeding and whether my thoughts on metaphors for God had yet been published. I thank her for her generosity of spirit and her empathic eye for the text as she edited this work.

Colleagues in the venues where ministry has taken me have been supportive in many different ways. When I first served the Mission Hills United Methodist Church in San Diego, parishioners not only were fascinated with my explorations, but some were willing to participate in small groups to help me think through implications of metaphors for God for my dissertation. A nearby pastor, Rev. Preston Price, saw the relevancy of challenging static God metaphors, and his dramatic, outrageous, forthright use of some of the ideas we discussed helped me to realize these ideas could be shared boldly with church congregations.

For twenty-one years professor colleagues at United Theological Seminary in Dayton, Ohio, were sources of insight and friendships as we mutually shared our disciplines and passions. Especially, I thank Andrew Sung Park, Larry Wellbourn, Kathy Farmer, Marsha Foster Boyd, and Ai Ra Kim. Students in seminary, most of whom were also serving small churches, were fabulous dialogue partners.

Back in the local church setting for five years at Aldersgate United Methodist Church in Orange County, California, I have shared plenty of these ideas with parishioners, and they have been gracious in their reflective responses. I thank especially George and Sally Puente. Virtually every Sunday, George shared thought-provoking comments with an affirming flair, and Sally sang from the Source of Divine Beauty.

For the past five years, my sister, Marilyn Collins, has listened over the phone to every sermon before I preached it, and she is radically honest with her responses. Plenty of the ideas in this book were clarified as I responded to her questions.

Our children, Alexandra and Stephen, are evident in many of the stories that appear in this book. How we think about God affects the next generation in huge ways. I thank them for their patience, their sharing, and their love.

John Cobb and Marjorie Suchocki are God's "Team Transformers" as they do all they can to embolden others to share and clarify theology in very practical ways. I am grateful that they so frequently kick the ball to other writers, including myself, encouraging us to communicate—for God's sake!

INTRODUCTION

A wise woman once told me about her predicament. Until a few years earlier, she had written stories with characters that came fully alive for her. She also had a rich array of metaphors for God that would be there for her—or she would be able to let arise—as she experienced God in different ways. However, a physical illness caused her to lose her creative imaging. She knew right away that the fictional characters were no longer so alive within her, but it was only gradually that she realized her ability to imagine God in significantly meaningful ways had faded, too. This was cause for great grieving, for she had enjoyed thinking of God as Roots of the Big Tree or Dancing Presence—metaphors that would evoke genuine wonder.

In the midst of our conversation, she shared something significant: she believed that if we consider ourselves "made in the image of God," the "image" we share in common with God is to be "image makers," to be able to create, to visualize, to imagine. For her, this (hopefully temporary) loss of ability to imagine dulled her connection with God.

Our discussion and her soul bearing moved me. She helped me to treasure even more than I had already our human ability to envision God.

Though our metaphors for God are not formal descriptions, there is no way to think of God without metaphors. Our metaphors point to the God we believe in, and *the pointing is experiencing.* If we "point" emotionally, mentally, and spiritually to God as Comforter, then we are likely to experience comfort. If we point to God as Taskmaster, we might experience demands from God. Trusting that God is helping us in the process, we can listen, touch, and look all around us, joyously and expectantly ready to find and experience God.

Though no human imaginings can capture God's essence, how we think about God affects us. For example, the gender we have tucked into our metaphor for God affects not only how we think about God, but also how we think about males and females. During an avalanche of interest in gender metaphors for God, I wrote a book, *Prayer on Wings,*[1] in which I made long lists of metaphors for God that were feminine, masculine, androgynous, and gender-free. However, over time I have realized that implicit gender in the God metaphor may not be what matters most. Whether our God is Mother or Father in our naming, what affects our beliefs or prayers is how we imagine God to have and use *power,* how God *wills* and makes God's will happen—or not. What matters for our faith is how we, God, and the world *relate* to each other. What of suffering? How does God care?

If you are a person who wonders about God, you may have come to logical conclusions about what you believe. Nevertheless, you might place all this aside when you allude to God with a metaphor. For example, you may believe that humans have freedom in relation to God, that humans can make mistakes and go against the "will" of God. However, if you pray or sing to God the Potter, you implicitly identify yourself as clay, even though clay has minimal freedom in relation to the Potter.

Metaphors matter. We may be shocked at how much.

I thought I knew what I believed about God. I had gone to seminary, earned a PhD, taught in a seminary, and written a good deal about God. Then, in 1994, I was near the epicenter of an earthquake in Northridge, California. That jarred my "gut-God" as no logical thinking had. I faced ambiguity squarely. God did not become distant, cruel, or unclear; actually, God became more vivid, more realistic. In many ways, my faith became more "grown-up." God remained compassionate, but I became even more passionate that we humans consider our responsibility in relation to this world.

Change occurred in my lived faith again in 2003, when our son died an accidental death when he was almost nineteen. Devastated, I found that one previously meaningful way of thinking of God, as Mother Eagle who carries her young ones on her wings until they can fly well themselves, became painfully inaccurate. I wish God could have carried our son until he was safe. I wish God could have saved him, though I do believe that God was trying to persuade everyone in the circumstance to choose more wisely. I still speak of God, preach about God, pray to God, but now all metaphors are nuanced because of this loss.

The metaphor of God as Jazz Band Leader is exceptionally relevant for me right now. It fits with a good deal of what I believe. This metaphor came to my rescue after the earthquake and still hangs around. The Jazz Band Leader God nods to me to do my riff—to share my passionate views on the significance of exploring God metaphors, for example. The Jazz Band Leader God also helps me enjoy life with others as we improvise our way forward, with God making meaningful music alongside us, and maybe, too, within us. Love and Creative-Nurturing God also point to the Divine for me as I face life's pain and hopes. Still other metaphors for God will be born as my faith continues to mature.

I invite you to share in this journey of faith. My passion is not to get you to believe in God in a certain way; I leave that to God. Rather, my passion is to name *options* for considering God.

For centuries, humans have tried to identify their experience of God in words. At the checkout stand at my local bookstore, a tiny deck of cards bears the name *The 72 Names of God: Meditation Deck.*[2] Inside are cards with names such as Silent Partner,

Umbilical Cord, and DNA of the Soul—ways to meditate upon God from a kabbalistic perspective. In the Islamic faith, creating images of Allah is forbidden, but in the Qur'an it is said, "And if all the trees in the earth were pens and the ocean (were ink), with seven oceans behind it to add to its (supply), yet would not the words of God be exhausted (in the writing): for God is Exalted in Power, full of Wisdom" (31:27). In the Christian faith, Jesus sought to alter some of the lived God metaphors of his day, from God as a Lawmaker to a more familiar Abba (Daddy), a Woman Looking for a Coin, and a Shepherd attending to sheep. Jesus also identified himself as a Mother Hen, caring for Jerusalem, and he said, "I and the Father are one" (John 10:30).

Not all metaphors are helpful—for an individual or for humanity. We are not dealing with only personal images that make us feel good, but with images that reveal how God's power and responsibility connect with our own. Even if a person does not believe in God, the metaphor for the God she or he does not believe in matters, for it can affect how she or he lives with others and the earth. For those who do believe in God, it is important to consider what the implications of our metaphors are. If we settle for only one metaphor for God, we limit our potential experience of God. I believe the converse is also true: if we expand our metaphors for God, we expand our experience of God.

What images come to your mind when you think of God? Has your image changed over the years, in varying circumstances? How much is your image of God in sync, or out of sync, with your beliefs about God? The search for authentic metaphors for God is really a search for what you believe about God.

The metaphors presented in this book are images I have considered at some point in my own devotional practice, or that I have explored with other people who were searching for congruence between their thoughts of God and their spiritual practice.

As you consider the metaphors discussed here, I invite you to explore them with others in a small group or class. You can use the Discussion Guide at the end of the book to examine new possibilities together. I also encourage you to use the God Belief and God Metaphor Checklists to do your own "metaphor wondering." I have included three checklists: one to use *before* you read this book, a second to use *after* your reading, and a third to use at a later date, so you can see how your metaphors shift over time.

May this book awaken new realms in your God experience. May it lead you to discover new facets of your God relationship. May it help you to envision both what is and what could be.

Before you start to read this book, take a look at the God Belief Checklist on page 133. If you spend a few minutes now to fill out this checklist, you will have a record of where you are in your current thinking about God, what God can do, what God wants, and how God relates to humans. After you have finished reading the book, fill out God Metaphor Checklist 1 to see if any of your thinking about God has shifted, as well as to consider which metaphors for God are compatible with your beliefs.

1

God the *What*?

A LIVELY, MULTIDIMENSIONAL FAITH

Consider how our views of God take on multi-dimensions. If we stand in one spot for a very long time, believing, let's say, in God as Judge, we might eventually lose our balance. Suppose something happens, we observe an amazing healing and are deeply grateful to God. God as Judge is still there (we can go back to that spot), but we now have a second meaningful way to think about God, as Miracle Worker, as One who will answer prayer.

We may hold these two images until one day we encounter someone who has a different view, who thinks of God as Friend, as One who may not perform miracles, but who is totally committed to being with us on all our journeys, no matter what. We may remain simply informed about this possibility and choose to stick with our Judge and Miracle Worker images. Or, we may add a new dimension to our experience of God, not only expecting either judgment or answers to prayers, but also enjoying the presence of an Infinite Friend.

Secure in our faith with God as Friend, sometimes Miracle Worker, and sometimes Judge, we might be content ... until, one day, someone talks of God as his or her Dance Partner! This person does not blame God for the tragedies in his or her life, but finds in God the courage to move forward, even to dance.

We could say that God takes on many dimensions. I think God even helps to reveal new dimensions to us, when we need them. If or when we have what *we* call "unbelief," maybe what is happening is that we are entering a new dimension. Maybe we are about to discover God in a way that brings new meaning, even more joy, to our lives.

The point is, we do not have to let go of one sense of God to take up another. Neither do we need to go about challenging old metaphors. What is crucial is to find a metaphor—or two, or six—that creatively point toward what we believe. We might still think of God as Judge, while God as Dance Partner helps us to have a lively, multidimensional faith.

People in ancient days were not so different from us. They had living faiths, just like us, and this is mirrored in the collage of hundreds of views of God we find in the Judeo-Christian Bible. They believed in God within the assumptions of their day, and sometimes they questioned that very God. What comes down to us are not theological debates but accounts of their experience of the Divine.

In various locations in the Bible, God is referred to with different names and metaphors, as Rock, Daddy, Miracle Worker, Mother Hen, Consoler, and Creator. Yet, there is seldom a debate in which people ask each other:

"Is God more like a Rock, steady and steadfast, or a Daddy, ready to come to our aid and to teach us wisely?"

"Is God more like a Miracle Worker, taking bad things that happen and making us better again—or a Visitor who shows up now and then with blessings?"

"Is God more like a Mother Hen who gathers tiny spring chicks under her wings to protect them from any harm, or like a soaring Eagle who helps the eaglets learn to fly, swooping down to catch them if they have not yet passed flight school?"

"Is God a Consoler, helping us when we are dismayed, or a powerful Judge—watching our every action to assign us to heaven or hell?"

"Is God the One who created the beautiful earth, but also the instigator of earthquakes, volcanoes, and tidal waves?"

We find these different ways of thinking of God as we read about biblical people who described their experiences of God in ways that made sense to them at the time.

In Genesis 18:1–8, for example, three visitors show up at Abraham's tent. The narrator tells us these visitors are God and two angels, but Abraham looks at the three beings and thinks they are three men. Fortunately for Abraham, he is quite hospitable to the three.

There is no theological debate in this account, but a theological perspective has been presented: God is understood as being able to walk on Earth and to be experienced by other humans as a person. This down-to-earth theology is typical of what biblical scholars call the Jahwist source material in the Hebrew Bible.[1] With this view, God is referred to as "YHWH" (Yahweh), and is imaged to walk on Earth, to be a personal presence. In other parts of the Hebrew Bible, which derive from other source material, God is called by other names—Elohim, for example—and is not expected to be so humanlike, engaging with people on Earth.

We find another view of God, God as Miracle Worker, in the story of Jesus healing a boy who had an affliction (Matt. 17:14–21; Mark 9:14–29; Luke 9:37–43a). This view is implicit in a piece of the dialogue between Jesus and the boy's father. The father says, "If you are able to do anything, have pity on us and help us." Jesus responds, "All things can be done for the one who believes." Immediately the father cries out, "I believe;

help my unbelief!" (Mark 9:22–24). While Jesus did the healing in this story, the implication for us is that God the Healer or Miracle Worker will heal today, if we have enough faith.

Whether we look through the window of historical faith or into the mirror at ourselves (and at each other), we see many references to God that seem natural to people who are describing their faith. The way we experience God is summed up quite succinctly in the metaphors we use.

WHAT MAKES A GOOD METAPHOR?

Some of the best metaphors in literature or common parlance are metaphors that startle us or shock us into an insight. The word *metaphor* comes from Greek and means "a transfer," or "to carry over, to transfer." In other words, metaphors describe what "carries over" between two unrelated objects, even though one object, at first, may not seem connected to the other. The surprise comes in seeing the two in relationship to each other. The insight is that the object that is least able to be described may have some characteristics of the object that can more clearly be known.

Two elements are essential for a good metaphor. First, it has to convey both *similarities* and *differences* between the thing and the more abstract object to which it points. Second, it has to be relevant.

The first point is crucial. For a metaphor to be viable—creatively enticing us to understand its intent—it needs to evoke a double response in us, both a, "Yes, it is like that," and a, "No, it is not."[2] For example, when we read a poem that describes fog as coming in on "little cat feet,"[3] we know that the fog has no feet whatsoever. However, we can amusingly nod in agreement, "Yes, the fog *is* coming in silently—like a cat does—but, no, the fog does *not* have feet." Or, when we speak of "a sky-blue sweater," we mean that the color is very much like that of the sky, but we also realize that the color is not *exactly* like that of sky. For one thing, the sky changes color, and the sweater does not.

Every meaningful metaphor implies some *differences* between the thing and that to which it points. When a metaphor suggests something quite the opposite of what we think, it can evoke a negative reaction that might actually help us clarify the objects under consideration. Say, for example, a friend calls my jacket "cloudy white." At first, I consider the comparison an insult, believing she thinks my jacket is unclean. When I react to her comment, she explains that she is referring to the jacket's fluffiness. Her metaphor mixed me up; it was not an apt metaphor, but our further conversation clarifies the matter.

These same dynamics apply to God metaphors. To be useful, a metaphor for God needs to evoke both reactions *at the same time:* "Oh, yes, God *is* like that," and, "Well, no, God is *not* quite like that." A God metaphor is not an effective metaphor for us if our response is *only* "Yes," or *only* "No." If we say God is like a Rock, we probably are referring to God being steady, always there, strong; however, we are not saying that God is made of granite or limestone, and I certainly do not think we mean God is unable to feel. The image of a Rock is a good metaphor to use occasionally for God, but it *is* a metaphor. God is *like* a Rock, in some ways, and *not* in others.

If our "No" reaction is simply a mild disclaimer, that is actually what *should* happen in response to a good metaphor. God is *not* like every metaphor we use, even metaphors we appreciate and use frequently. God is not like a Potter, a Father, a Lord, a Mother in myriad ways—not the least of which is that all of those metaphors are anthropomorphic, making God's image like our own. We know God is not like humans in many ways.

Since this point is so important, I will say it again in another way. Sometimes we find a good metaphor that explains something not so well known (such as God) in terms of something well known (such as a Daddy). However, we should also feel some element of surprise whenever we hear a really good and helpful metaphor. Given that we appreciate the metaphor, we should still be able to say, "Well, it is not precisely like that."

It is equally important that we do not *equate* the two things being compared by a metaphor. A metaphor should not be taken as the thing itself; it is not to be understood literally. It would be naïve to search for clouds in sweaters and jackets or cats' feet in fog! Similarly, we should not *equate* God with Potter, Father, Lord, or Mother.

The second criterion, if a metaphor is to make any sense, is that it has to be relevant. If you had never seen little cat's feet, fluffy clouds, or a blue sky, you would have no idea how to interpret what is meant when those metaphors are used to refer to fog or clothing. If a metaphor seems too absurd and infers a similarity we do not comprehend, it just does not work. For example, if a friend says, "The fog comes in on a flying saucer," I might scratch my head in confusion. The metaphor is not illuminating because I do not know how a flying saucer "comes in"! The metaphor tells me nothing helpful about the fog. In order to understand the metaphor, I need to know something about its referent.

This principle of relevancy also applies to God metaphors—they need to be relevant to our lives if they are to be helpful. A metaphor that is irrelevant to us will not work, for we will not get the connection. For example, if someone says God is like a Palm Tree, I do not personally see the connection (even though there are plenty of such trees where I live in Southern California). What about people who have never even seen a palm tree? The palm tree metaphor for God would be meaningless for them. Yet, for those whose lifestyle includes enjoying fresh dates or coconuts from palm trees, this metaphor may be far more relevant than a well-used biblical metaphor, such as God the Shepherd. The bottom line is that it would be absurd to think that we could find one metaphor that would actually capture the way God is. Yet, metaphors—if neither equated with God nor irrelevant—can truly expand our understanding of the Divine.

The challenge, then, becomes discovering which metaphors limit, or conflict, with our sense of God, and which metaphors revitalize or increase our perception. I have been exploring God metaphors these many years, and I am still amazed at what people come up with when they think about God in creative ways, and how those images invigorate their faith. In the next three sections, you will meet people who discovered new meaning in familiar metaphors; people who ran into problems with particular God metaphors and challenged those; and people who invented wonderful, quirky metaphors for God that enlivened their spiritual life.

What works for you may be totally different from the metaphors presented here, but the important thing to keep in mind as you read about the "metaphor wondering" of these people is that metaphors—whether traditional or unique—*point*. The best metaphors point toward God in creative ways that ring true.

BRINGING NEW MEANING TO OLD METAPHORS

Shepherd
Potter
Author
Daddy
Love
Rock
Seamstress
Repairer

None of these metaphors are new ways of conceiving of God. They were not discovered as twenty-first-century people searched for relevant metaphors. These metaphors are old, ancient, yet as we learn about their origins and meanings, they can be vital images for us today as we link spiritual hands with those centuries ago who sought to name how they related to the Divine.

God the Shepherd

Depending on our particular culture, when we need comfort food, we eat tomato soup, chicken soup with noodles, meatloaf and mashed potatoes, hot cocoa, rice, warm tortillas, or coconut. When we need comfort, we may listen to soft music, take a warm bath, walk along a mountain path or the beach, or stay in bed with the covers tightly around us. When we need comfort and turn to the Bible, many of us are inclined to turn to Psalm 23:

The Lord is My Shepherd, I shall not want.
He makes me lie down in green pastures;
he leads me beside still waters; he restores
my soul.
He leads me in right paths for his name's sake.
Even though I walk through the darkest valley,
I fear no evil; for you are with me;
your rod and your staff—they comfort me.
You prepare a table before me in the presence of
my enemies;
you anoint my head with oil;
my cup overflows
Surely goodness and mercy shall follow me
all the days of my life,
and I shall dwell in the house of the Lord my
whole life long.

Green pastures, still waters, not wanting for anything, a restored soul, no fear, an overflowing cup, anointment with oil, and assurance of goodness and mercy every day of our lives—what comfort!

For most of my life, I was so attuned to the King James translation of the phrase, "Yea, though I walk through the valley of the shadow of death" (Ps. 23:4a) that I thought of this psalm as mostly relevant for funerals. Our family—like many—read this psalm at our mother's memorial service. Now I see that the psalm is an affirmation of the goodness of life and a statement of unconditional trust in God. It is filled with images of immense comfort for *living*.

Clearly, the psalmist likens God to a Shepherd. However, when a colleague pointed out to me that the whole psalm is told entirely from a *sheep's* perspective, my understanding of the psalm zoomed. Shepherd as a relevant metaphor for me underwent a transformation.

How often do we humans lie down in green pastures? We might enjoy lying down occasionally on the grass in our backyards, but green pastures? Do you long to be led beside still waters? Would those images of green pastures and still waters come first to your mind if you were looking for comfort? We might long for cozy beds and for good friends, but *pastures* and *still water?* No. Sheep long, if they long at all, for those things.

From the sheep's perspective, the valley of the shadow of death was a real place in Palestine, a natural valley south of Jericho that led from Jerusalem to the Dead Sea. It was a very narrow path through a mountain range that shepherds and their sheep needed to traverse in order to get to the feeding ground. The sidewalls of the valley were over fifteen hundred feet high in places, and the journey was about four and one-half miles long. The footing on the path was so narrow that in many places sheep could not turn around. In fact, there was an unwritten code in ancient days that the flocks would go up the valley in the morning and down toward eventide, or else there would be enormous confusion.

At night, the shepherd prepares a sheepfold, a shelter for the sheep to sleep in. The shepherd has an overflowing container of oil for the sheep and, each night, inspects every animal for bruises or snags, gently massaging the sheep with olive oil, never sparing the oil. If sheep trip at the edge of a narrow path, the shepherd encircles the sheep's neck with the crook of his or her rod and assists it to safety ("your rod and your staff—they comfort me," Ps. 23:4b).

Evidently, it is the temperament of sheep that they will not drink from a gurgling stream or a noisy current of water. They need *still* waters. Hence, the Shepherd "leads me beside still waters" (Ps. 23:3a).

A Basque herder named Ferdinando DeAlfonso offers an explanation of one of the most puzzling lines of this psalm—"You prepare a table before me in the presence of my enemies" (Ps. 23:5–6b). DeAlfonso thinks the "enemies" refered to in this line are actually poisonous plants! Plants that are fatal to grazing animals grow around the Holy Land, and DeAlfonso explains that the shepherds are constantly on guard for these poisonous plants in the feeding grounds. The shepherd digs out every poisonous stalk and leads the sheep to their newly prepared "table"—a pasture that has been cleaned of enemy plants—so they can eat in peace.[4]

If we were sheep, God would be like a Shepherd to us. That is the whole point. That is the major point: God is attentive, providing safety, shelter, and healing, giving us what we really need.

When we consider the Shepherd metaphor, we need to keep in mind the criterion that makes a metaphor work: does it generate a double response ("Yes," and "No, not exactly")? Shepherd, as a metaphor for God, has met with a resounding, "Yes, God is like that!" for hundreds of years because it creates a sense of comfort. Shepherd God is helpful, observant, and always there. Yet, we are not sheep. We are human beings who have the capacity for even more delight than sheep.

We also have the capacity to imagine ourselves to be sheep.

Once, when I taught Sunday school in Dayton, Ohio, I led our class outside. We lay down on the grass, listening to and reading this psalm, thinking of ourselves as sheep. Then we tried to think of the same idea from various perspectives. One child wrote from the perspective of the sheepfold, the shelter; another wrote from the grass's perspective.

This psalm is a powerful statement of faith about God. It states what most of us *want* to believe about God, that God provides, helps us to have food, water, and rest; God restores us, cares for us in the narrow passages of our lives, makes us not need to fear, even helps us to discern poisonous plants; God is always with us.

Yet, obviously, everyone around the world does not have enough food or rest. Some people *do* live in fear. Some people *do* eat poisonous plants. We need to recognize that this psalm is a hymn, a prayer to God, *not* a statement of reality. Though the metaphor of Shepherd points to God, we can easily say, "God is not exactly like that everywhere, all the time, for all people," especially if we highlight the necessity for human wisdom and responsibility in conjunction with God's caretaking. This psalm challenges us to ponder anew what we think about our experience of God.

Personally, I do not believe that God spares us from all that we can get ourselves into; but God tries so darn hard. With every step we take, God tries to keep us on the path of wisdom. God tries to get our attention and to weed out the dangers for many health hazards.

There is something about Psalm 23 that invites translations, remakes, and thinking from other perspectives. When I checked the Internet, I found dozens of musical renditions, plenty of images, and various translations, with names such as "The 23rd Psalm for Busy People."[5]

You might consider writing your translation or remake of this psalm, from your own perspective. Using the Shepherd God metaphor, you could write from the perspective of the oil, the rod, or the path. Alternatively, you could find a completely different metaphor for yourself as a human being seeking comfort. If you believe that God can help you to be or to feel safe and calm, what metaphor for God would evoke that trust?

When I suggested to a group that they rewrite this psalm, or parts of it, in ways that would give them comfort, two people took me up on it. A woman friend who had a newborn baby sent me an e-mail with her very relevant version of some lines of this psalm. She wrote that God was feminine for her right now: "God is Mother, I am sustained. God helps me lie down for much needed sleep ..." A college student scribbled a note and mailed it to me, with this idea: "God is my Wise Counselor, pointing out paths to take."

I can just imagine that some people's translations might start, "God is my Caddy ..."

God the Divine Potter, the Divine Author

Our son is the only potter I know. He took a couple of years of pottery classes in high school, and I am grateful for the pottery he created, as well as for his sharing with me some of his process. As he thought about what to make at school, it dawned on him that a communion chalice would be a great gift for me, and he announced that he was working on it. It took a while, but one day he finally brought it home. I hugged it, and him, but I did need to name the fact that it was rather large (for serving communion, that is). When I have used it in serving Holy Communion, I have announced that it holds God's crazy big love, God's huge grace. Stephen said he knew the chalice was a bit big, but "it is hard to start small.... What size do you want?"

Sometimes Stephen would pick up a piece of pottery he had made and just hold it. He would turn it in his hand, caressing it, remembering how it was to make it, to turn it.

Can you imagine yourself as the pottery of God, with God's hands caressing you, remembering your turning? Can you imagine being in God's hands as God enjoys who you are now?

Two biblical passages—one from the book of the prophet Isaiah and one from Paul's letter to the early Christian community at Ephesus—speak of us humans as the works of God. These passages affirm, in various translations, that "we are the work of God's hands" (Isa. 64:8), or "we are what God made us" (Eph. 2:10). One way we can imagine being the handiwork of God is to think of ourselves as the clay and God as the Potter. These passages can also evoke the image of God as Artisan, Craftsperson, even Author or Poet.

What if we took these passages with utmost seriousness? It could go to our heads, realizing that we are the creations of God! We could get puffed up about this phenomenon. After all, God does good work. Yet, it is *also* true that we are "works in progress"—God's works in progress, but still, in progress. Some of us have been fired by life's intense heat. Some of us are colorful; others are earthier. Yet, the patient turning of the Divine Potter has made us all, spinning us around, shaping us, handling us gently, firmly, and creatively. Sometimes we may be well centered, so that God's hands are able to mold us quite to God's will. Sometimes, though, we might best be described as "all wet"!

If we were to consider ourselves the handiwork of God the Author, we could imagine ourselves as God's poetry or prose. Maybe some of us feel like first drafts, while others sense that they have gone through many revisions and have been transformed by the Author's arduous task of expressing exactly what the Author intends to say.

I vividly remember the ending of the oral exam that was almost the last step in my final degree. One of the professors at the exam asked me about my writing process. He commented that, with "a few more drafts," I might be able to publish my dissertation. "A few more drafts" was all that I heard. Did he realize that I had already made a complete revision, that this was already draft number two? I had made the necessary changes! What was he talking about, "a few more drafts"? Then the professor, whom I admired greatly and whose books I had read, commented that usually it took him four to six drafts to manage to say what he meant. Four to six drafts?

That moment totally transformed my notion of writing, and I completely agree with him now. It often takes me six drafts to say what I mean.

When I began preaching about forty years ago, almost every Sunday afternoon I would think about what I had *meant* to say that morning but did not quite say. I now realize that the main reason I had those ideas "after the fact" was that I had preached what, in essence, was my first draft. Nowadays, I start working on sermons way before Saturday. In fact, what the congregation hears is usually my third draft. It is still a work in progress, but it is much closer to what I mean than the sermons I used to preach.

In the book of Isaiah, a verse in the middle of a long poem that was carefully crafted over a number of years (I am sure there were many oral and written drafts of this poem!) declares, "We are the clay, and you are our potter; we are all the work of your hand" (Isa. 64:8). This poem just may be so carefully crafted that it actually says what it means!

Some of us are probably third or fourth drafts of God's poetry. Maybe some of us are ninth drafts. What is the use of more and more drafts? What is the reason for such a long time on the Divine Potter's wheel?

When writers compose poems, the purpose of multiple drafts is to achieve two things: to say what they mean and to create something beautiful. When potters throw a pot, the purpose of a second or third try is to make something both useful and lovely. So what about *us*? Is not what God did with us on the first draft good enough? Was not the Divine Potter's first attempt sufficient? Why do we have so much improving to do? Why are we works in progress—usually able to improve in so many ways? Why should we make the effort to be more loving, to be more true to ourselves, to be more useful, if God made us as we are to begin with?

We talk about purchasing items "Made in the U.S.A." In California we see signs that read *"Hecho en México"* (Made in Mexico). If we think of God as the Divine Artisan, then you and I—and all of our fellow humans—are *hecho en Dios,* "made in God." How to accept ourselves as we are, *hecho en Dios,* and how to stay alert to being a "work in progress," ready to be edited or colored or fired is a challenging balance act.

Both the Divine Author and Divine Potter metaphors can lead us to consider that God is an Artisan who *enjoys* being creative, who likes to edit, mold, and shape us. This is a fun way of thinking of how God keeps working on us. As John Wesley, the founder of Methodism, used to say, we are "going on to perfection." Maybe the way we can motivate ourselves to keep improving is to consider ourselves to be *living more and more closely to what God means to express through us.* We can think of our self-improvement as a partnership. God is editing us, or we are letting God, the Author of Life Divine, edit us. Maybe when we are close to being a final draft, we are close to what God is trying to create through us.

God the Father—"My Daddy"

Visualize this: You are at Disneyland, or some other amusement park, amid thousands of fun-seekers on a hot summer day. You are waiting in line. After all, is that not what we do when we seek fun—wait in line? In front of you is a man. You see a little arm flopping, sliding off the man's shoulder. A toddler's head is plunked against the man's neck. The toddler is asleep, limp, relaxed, at peace, held by the man who is probably his father.

The child is dependent upon the dad to be held, to be given comfort, to be allowed a chance to rest, and to be protected. Yet, there is something more in that view of the little arm flopping over the man's shoulders: *love*.

Sometimes it is wonderful to think of God like that dad, comforting us, protecting us, and loving us.

Visualize this: A five-year-old is on his way to kindergarten. He has a lunch box in one hand. With the other, he reaches over and takes the hand of his daddy. The dad accepts the little hand, and they walk on to the school. The young boy says, "Bye, Daddy-o," kissing him. Daddy-o winks; they squeeze hands and let go.

Sometimes it is helpful to think of God as One to whom we can reach out or up when we are heading toward new adventures.

Visualize this: A fourteen-year-old girl is making a transition, from slow-pitch to fast-pitch softball. In the new league, she has to slide into second base, or—under even more pressure—slide into home plate! Her father never slid into a base in his life, but he has watched a lot of baseball. He knows some of the do's and don'ts. He understands it is scary to throw your body forward on the ground. He takes his daughter to soft grass to practice after everyone else has left the field. He says, "Go," and she does. She slides into the base. So excited, she wants to do it again … and again. He teases her, and says he is proud of her.

Sometimes it is encouraging to think of God as the dad who says, "Go, girl!" dozens, hundreds of times, not fretting over failures.

The dad who carries the peacefully plunked toddler on his shoulder, the Daddy-o who accepts his son's hand on the way to school, and the father who teaches his teenager to slide are comforting, challenging, and empowering images. God is, we can imagine, like all these dads in some ways. Therefore, when we name God, we may understandably call God "Father."

Usually when people pray to God the Father, they do not actually *imagine* a man in front of them in line providing rest for a toddler. However, the fact that so many people pray to Father implies that much about this metaphor for God is helpful; it evokes the *experience* of the Spiritual Presence. I suggest that it is quite okay to expand this metaphor. If you call God "Daddy," for heaven's sake, let yourself *imagine* God as daddy!

The musical *Mamma Mia* uses the music of the pop group ABBA. I understand the band's name was created from the initials of the first names of the group's members. The term *Abba,* however, is actually the Aramaic word for "Daddy." Jesus used the word *Abba* when he prayed what Protestants call the Lord's Prayer and Roman Catholics call the Our Father (Matt. 6:9b–13, Luke 11:2–4). If we were being more true to the words Jesus actually prayed, we would begin the prayer, "Our Daddy, who is in heaven."

I do not know how a man feels when he is called daddy, but I carry around in my datebook a little note that accompanied a birthday gift from our daughter. It reads, "I love you, Mommy." Since she was twenty-three when she wrote the note, her calling me "Mommy" was quite endearing to me.

Jesus, I imagine, used the term *Daddy* very intentionally. Jesus was a rabbi who inherited the Hebrew tradition that held a cluster of references for God. The unutterable name for God that we find translated as Yahweh and the reference to God as Elohim are today both often translated as "the Lord." We sometimes see God called King. The Psalms occasionally referred to God as Rock. Jesus introduced the name Daddy. A King or Lord gives orders and makes things happen. A Daddy—*loves*! If our God is a God of love, if God *is* Love, then Daddy is a wonderful metaphor for God. Abba! Abba Mia, My Daddy.

How that metaphor transforms the feeling and tone of our relation to God! A wonderful consequence of thinking of God as

Daddy is implicit in the Lord's Prayer. By saying, "*Our* Father," Jesus names God to be *ours,* making us all siblings.

Even though the metaphor of God as Father holds much relevance for us, I personally, with the weekly exception of leading the Lord's Prayer in church, do not use this metaphor very often because it is the one that leads to the greatest confusion. Instead of being a metaphor that *points* toward a set of characteristics we believe God to have, this metaphor often becomes who God *is*.

To help grasp what I mean by this, picture this scene:

A woman is hanging a photo on the wall. She yells, "Honey, would you come in here and tell me if it's straight?" Her husband, Bill, arrives to help. Later, the woman wants to go for a walk. She asks, "Honey, would you like to go for a walk?" He says, "Sure." Later still, the woman sits down to dinner—which Bill has grilled, since this is in Southern California—and she says, "Thanks, Honey. This tastes great."

Why does the woman call Bill "Honey"? Honey is a great metaphor for her loved one because he is sweet and enjoyable. Is Bill, then, honey? Can she put him on toast, in her tea? Of course not. Bill is not actually honey. She calls her husband "Honey" because it is an endearing term. Notice, it is not just the case that Bill's *name* is not "Honey," but also *Bill* is not honey.

This woman could say, "Bill, who is like honey, would you come in here and tell me if this picture is straight?" She could say, "Bill, who reminds me of honey, would you like to go for a walk?" That sounds strange and is cumbersome. It loses some of its oomph. It is not so endearing. Let's face it; the woman is very unlikely to mistake her husband for honey, so this is not a problem.

It is not quite the same with God. Father is, for many people, a great metaphor for God. However, Father sometimes becomes God's name, even who God is. Father is not the *name* for God, neither *is* God a father. Yet, given our assumptions about fathers and about God, it is wonderful sometimes to think of God as Abba. God is *like* a Father, a Daddy, Abba Mia, My Daddy. Occasionally God and father are merged so that God becomes Father. Settling for any one metaphor for God can hinder our exploration of other aspects of our wonderfully complex relationship with God.

There is one more issue that comes up with the Daddy/Father metaphor—with any "human" metaphors, for that matter—and that is the association we make between our human fathers and our image of God acting with fatherly qualities.

Personally, I had a fine relationship with my earthly father, and, because of that, I can easily imagine God to be fatherlike at times. If I were to think of God as being like *my* father, I would have images of God defending me no matter what, giving me huge freedom, being very responsible, and being tenacious in his love.

Over the past years of ministry, I have heard people say that they have such a *wonderful* earthly father that they did not *need* a fatherly God. I have heard others say that they have such a *negative* father image that they do not *want* a Father God. I have heard still others say that they have had such a *negative* father image that they *need* a Father God. Moreover, I have heard others say that they had such a *great* father that they *love* to call God Father.

That leaves me with the conclusion that we cannot draw any one conclusion between earthly fathers and people's inclination to speak of God as Father. However, I do think that if we wean ourselves from *always* using that metaphor, then the image of God as Daddy can become meaningful again. Instead of God practically having the *name* Father—so much so that we barely *think* of what that means—we might actually have the joy of visualizing ourselves resting on God's shoulder, or being taught how to slide into base, or holding tightly to God's hand as we head off to new adventures.

God of Love

Visualize this conversation taking place in a hospital's family waiting room:

Jessie: My wife has been ill for two years. We keep praying and hoping that God will cure her. Our children need two parents; she's not old. Now, to be truthful, she's given up on God. He's not doing anything to heal her. We've tried everything we know to do.

Chaplain: Jessie, I realize that you're desperate. I know you've tried and you have prayed fervently.

J: We have.... Our whole family prays that God will intervene and cure her. But, to tell you the truth, we're getting bitter. We haven't even prayed in over a month.

C: How do you think of God? How did you address God, when you used to pray?

J: Well, just like anybody, "Lord, heal Cathy ..."

C: I'm wondering, maybe it'd be worthwhile to think about that God, that Lord. While there is only one God, it sometimes makes a difference how we think about that God—not to God, of course, but to us.

J: Well, sometimes we say, "Oh, Heavenly Father, perform a miracle."

C: The God you pray to—I mean, used to pray to—is pretty powerful, One who would interrupt Cathy's illness immediately, healing her instantly.

J: That's the promise of an Almighty God, isn't it?

C: I think instant healing is possible, but in my experience, I've seen healings—physical and spiritual—happen gradually a lot more often than instantly.

J: I don't care how gradual or instant ... I just want *healing.* I'm desperate! I need her.

C: Since it seems you're at your wits' end, may I suggest you try something else? It couldn't hurt.

J: What is it?

C: How about, for a week, you think of God as having a different kind of power. Now I don't think that God will change at all because of what we do this week; I'm just suggesting that we (I'll join you in this) think of God as Love, for a week.

J: Love?

C: Yes. Your love for Cathy is powerful. So is her love for you and the kids. Love is amazingly powerful, even though we can't see immediately what love does.

J: Of course, God is Love.

C: We could pray to God, knowing that God loves every cell of Cathy's body. We could think of Cathy's body as having the power to receive God's love receptively, responsively. We could imagine Love moving in and out of her, with her every breath.

J: It's worth a try. I know God is Love, but I've rather wanted a miracle.

C: Yes, and I'm not ruling out miracles. I just think that since you're at an impasse—even giving up—it wouldn't hurt, for a week, to drop the prayers or hopes for instant cures and to concentrate as much as possible on God's power as Love.

J: You've got a deal. Could the kids join in?

> *C:* Sure. I'll come by the room when they come to visit, so we can talk together about God as Love. You follow up with them, and with Cathy, explaining this one-week trial. We can also reflect on how concentrating on Love affects you and me, as well as Cathy.

Most of us have no trouble thinking about God as Love in everyday life, but when we get into a crisis, we may tend to think of God more as Miracle Worker. This shift is understandable and may be relevant and meaningful. However, sometimes it is spiritually healthy to return to the image of God as Love, to dwell on that, period. God as Love may help us focus on a larger picture, not exclusively on how we accept answers to prayer.

God, Like a Rock

"Like a rock"—that was a slogan used in Chevy truck commercials for more than ten years; it was one of longest-running television commercials in history. Think about it. What made a Chevy truck "like a rock"? Did not General Motors want us to trust that their trucks were dependable, strong, there for us, able to handle anything?

I confess I have never wanted a Chevy truck, or any truck, and though I want my car to be dependable and able to handle anything, I do not give cars much thought, so the slogan did not do much to persuade me about vehicles. One particular rock in my life, however, did help me to appreciate the comfort of rocklike dependability. It was in Ohio, a rock from which our family used to start—and end—hikes. When we would approach the end of our hike, tired, we would see "the rock," and we would often run to it, knowing exactly where we were—always sure that the huge seven-foot rock had not moved. It was dependable, there for us.

The slogan "like a rock" actually came from a song of that name by Bob Seger on his 1986 album. While Seger may have the copyright on the song, he was not the first to use this simile. The Bible is filled with references to God being like a Rock:

> Yet his bow remained taut, and his arms were made agile by the hands of the Mighty One of Jacob, by the name of the Shepherd, the Rock of Israel (Gen. 49:24).
>
> The Rock, his work is perfect, and all his ways are just. A faithful God, without deceit, just and upright is he (Deut. 32:4).
>
> You were unmindful of the Rock that bore you; you forgot the God who gave you birth (Deut. 32:18).
>
> There is no Holy One like the Lord, no one besides you; there is no Rock like our God (1 Sam. 2:2).
>
> Let the words of my mouth and the meditation of my heart be acceptable to you, O Lord, my rock and my redeemer (Ps. 19:14).
>
> To you, O Lord, I call; my rock, do not refuse to hear me, for if you are silent to me, I shall be like those who go down to the Pit (Ps. 28:1).
>
> Trust in the Lord forever, for in the Lord God you have an everlasting rock (Isa. 26:4).

Imaging the Divine to be like a Rock makes sense, for we tend to think of God's qualities much like those advertised by Chevy: God is comfortingly dependable, strong, able to handle anything, and always there for us.

I do not imagine that the metaphor of Rock would be as intimate a prayer partner as Daddy or Infinite Friend for most people, most of the time. However, if we are in chaotic times or on long journeys—symbolic or literal—we might find spiritual strength and solid ground by conceiving of God as big, bold, and steady, like a Rock.

God Who Stitches and Mends

Although many hymns refer to God with biblical images such as a Rock, a Fortress (Ps. 18:2), and a Fountain of Living Water (Jer. 17:13), and although people sometimes experience God as Judge (Ps. 7:8), one of the most common ways we think of God is as Creator. When we consider our world, each other, ourselves, ideas, and even compassion, we experience God as somehow involved in all this ongoing creativity. We can surely think of God the Creator as a Father or a Mother, but we might also insightfully think of this God as Author of Life or Poet of the Universe. We might compare God's creativity to musicians and think of God as Composer or Jazz Band Leader.

Yet another way to consider God's creativity is through the arts that involve clothing—sewing, weaving, knitting, and the like. Not surprisingly, given that clothing is a basic human need, God is imagined in the Bible as "making clothes" for humans to wear: "And the Lord God made garments of skins for the man and his wife, and clothed them" (Gen. 3:21). In one commentary on this verse, God is referred to as "tailoring." Could we not also refer to God as "sewing" our relationships with the thread of compassion, "stitching" our responsibility-laden lives with calm strength, even "embroidering" our days with beauty?

In the eloquent verses of Psalm 139, God is referred to as "knitting": "For it was you who formed my inward parts; you knit me together in my mother's womb.... My frame was not hidden from you, when I was being made in secret, intricately woven in the depths of the earth" (Ps. 139:13, 15).

If you grew up in a household where knitting or sewing was part of the fabric of everyday life, this metaphor for God may be rich with meaning for you. Our mother sewed for hours every day; fabric stores were familiar places for us. I, however, did not take on my mother's love for sewing or stitching. I could not sew as well or as fast as she could. In addition, there was one feature of these arts I hated—ripping out.

Errors may lend a unique beauty to our quilts and to our lives. I understand that in some traditions of quilt making, the quilter would intentionally insert a mistake into the quilt, to affirm that only God is perfect. The quilt would then reflect creation, which has flaws. When sewing, if your piece contains a big enough mistake (which there always seemed to be, for me), you have to rip out your work and redo it. My mother accepted ripping out as a natural part of the process. She was even tolerant of my changing sizes between the time she would fit me and the time I wore the clothes. "No problem, I'll just alter it." (Actually, she did not say "no problem"—that is contemporary jargon—but she *conveyed* to me that it was "no problem," which was what was important.)

I like the image of God as being tolerant, having to rip out and make alterations. I can even imagine, instead of a *confession booth*, an *alterations department* where God stitches, and then alters as needed. As with the pottery or poem metaphors, it is useful to think of ourselves as unfinished products. If we are the quilts of God's tiny stitches, we are in process; we are still being made, grouped, bound, and bound again, to one another.

Not only does God stitch and alter, but most certainly, God also mends. I did perform one act with my needle and thread after I was grown: when the stuffing was coming out of our children's toy animals, I mended and kissed those stuffed creatures with great care, out of gratitude for the comfort they provided our children. Maybe we can imagine ourselves being lifted to God, for God to mend, to kiss, and to comfort.

There is another kind of stitching—the kind doctors do when we humans get big enough cuts to need mending. Our son once tripped, at church actually, and needed some stitches beside his eye. The emergency room doctor was a very clever stitcher and mender. He first had Stephen practice screaming, to demonstrate how well he could scream. Then he asked Stephen to scream again while he administered a painkiller shot and then mended Stephen's eye. (At least I understand this is how it went, for I stepped out of the room at that moment.) I am imagining that God does not mind if we scream at times, when we need God's mending stitches. We can scream with sadness, with embarrassment, with loneliness, with pain, and I think God will very cleverly find ways to mend us while we scream.

Perhaps we could gain comfort by considering ourselves held on God's lap as God makes tiny, tiny stitches upon us over and over. The image may help us to find hope again in an area of our lives in which we are distraught; or to love again, even when we have been hurt before. The image might help us to try for yet another job if we are out of work, or help us to look at ourselves in the mirror when we are disappointed with ourselves. This metaphor presents God as truly intimate in our lives, stitch by stitch by stitch. Nothing is too small for God to be stitching, altering, or mending.

God the Repairer, the Restorer

Isaiah is a prophet who cared for his people when they were in dire straits. He called them to task and encouraged them to repair and restore their destroyed ruins. Although Isaiah called the *people* to do the repair work, I think it is appropriate to consider that God would help them. Think of the possibilities of "repairer of the breach" and "restorer of streets to live in" (Isa. 58:12) as metaphors for God! We could visualize God the Repairer working in our lives when we are devastated and God the Restorer bringing us to a new level.

When we lived in Dayton, Ohio, there was a time that we smelled gas for several months but could not determine the source of a leak. We hired several different persons to determine the problem; they looked all over our house. Finally, one man realized there was a leak in the pipe that was under the grass in our front yard; the leak was not inside the house. Once the source of the problem was fully discovered, wise men who were well trained in repairing such leaks made the pipe "as good as new."

Similarly, we have problems in our lives that do not reveal their source easily. God the Repairer and Restorer may be a way of visualizing divine assistance as we do what we can to gain help from wise persons to find the problem and fix it.

Other times we can see exactly where the problem lies, but cannot imagine a way to fix it. At the church where I served in Orange County, an iron gate at the edge of our playground was broken. I recall with fascination the trustee meeting when we adjourned to the playground to analyze the situation. I watched three different men, with various professional backgrounds, figuring out the problem, how the gate was broken, and what to do to fix it. I had only thought, "The gate is broken and needs to be fixed." The real situation was far more complex than I had dreamed. Yet, these men restored the gate to its original function; even more, they repaired it in such a way that it would be more difficult to break again.

Broken relationships. Broken dreams. God the Repairer and Restorer may be quite a partner as solutions we could not have even imagined emerge to help mend the broken areas of our lives. If we remain open, the things that we think need to be replaced—a new friend, now that we lost an old one; a new dream, now that the dream we had has faded—may, in fact, be restored in a completely different, more complex, and marvelous manner.

Even as whole cities—such as New Orleans, and vast areas around the world that have been devastated by cyclones, hurricanes, tidal waves, or earthquakes—set to repairing and restoring their buildings and their lives after horrendous events, the metaphor of God the Repairer makes sense. God the Restorer may be a good way to imagine God's help when we desperately need not only individual, but also collective restoration.

METAPHOR WONDERING

Many people find a metaphor for God that fits with their beliefs and hang on to it. Sometimes we are raised with metaphors that we never outgrow: God as Father or God as Shepherd may make sense for us from the time we first hear those metaphors until we are ninety-two-years-old. But many of us find ourselves shedding certain metaphors, for a while at least, often because of a crisis of faith or a leap of insight that makes us question, then outgrow, an earlier metaphor.

The vignettes in this section present faith crises of four different individuals. One is a remembrance of my dad, who was in his seventies at the time; another is a middle-aged husband; the third is a young boy; and the final, a teenage girl. What these four had in common were periods of what I call "metaphor wondering." The ways the two men *assumed* God to be caused them faith frustrations—either they could no longer believe, or they faced what seemed like a dead end in prayer. The boy and girl were told something about God—through metaphors used by ministers—and were outraged by the implications of what they were taught. All four people wondered aloud and to others. In the conversations that emerged, they questioned what their metaphors revealed about their beliefs about God.

The God *Not* to Believe In

This first vignette comes from dialogue with my dad. In my mid-twenties, after I had been ordained, I visited my parents and took the opportunity to walk with my father on his early-morning hikes. Repeatedly, my father said to me, "Now that you're a minister, tell me how to believe. I do not believe in God. Why would God let me have all this pain, for years?" Sometimes he would say, "I don't believe in God. There just is not any hell, fire, and damnation after death. I don't believe that."

I told him that I did not believe in the God he did not believe in, either! I wanted desperately to help my dad grasp that if he wanted to believe, there were other ways of thinking of God that might make more sense to him. He did not need to keep rejecting the God with whom he grew up; he could explore a different image than a hellfire-and-damnation Judge. I also suggested that God did not have to be responsible for his pain, that many factors went into his suffering—genetics, childhood family dynamics, professional disappointments, myriad instances of unfairness, and varied environmental influences. I floated the idea that God could be suffering *with* him, not *making* him suffer. I even suggested that God could be trying to help him to think of new ways to consider God.

After I poured out all the ideas that had influenced me so profoundly in seminary, we arrived back at my parents' apartment, where he said, "Well, I just don't believe. I hate to tell you that, but I don't."

At the time, I was reading Anglican Bishop John Robinson's *Honest to God,*[6] in which Robinson challenges the belief in a God "out there," opting instead for what I once called in a sermon a "Down Here, Right Now God." That was a little of what I was trying to say to my dad. I was not trying to get him to "believe in God." In fact, I never brought up the subject of God. Because of his own disappointment in his God, he kept raising the issue. I began to consider that he needed to hold on to a particular God *not* to believe in. I wanted to show him that believing could mean something other than believing in the God that he did *not* believe in, that with a different image in mind, perhaps he could experience God "down here, right now."

The "How Great Thou Art" God

George, a man in his early fifties, went to his pastor after considering his difficulty of five months. He had thought long and hard about whether to bother the minister and to make himself vulnerable by telling the clergyman about his concern. However, his problem had not diminished and he felt desperate; he decided to risk it.

George told the pastor about not sleeping well and not having much zest for work or family—even for food or sex. George said he felt odd, unlike himself. The minister, who had some knowledge of counseling, thought he heard symptoms of depression. He recommended that George consult a physician, consider exercise, and use positive phrases to offer himself encouragement. In addition, the minister pointed out that people have periods when they need megadoses of being well heard, when they can benefit from having an empathy partner. The pastor volunteered to be that partner for George. "I'll listen to you, letting you know what I hear, over a period of a couple of weeks; then we'll see how you are doing."

About the third time they got together to talk, the pastor commented, "I know you are involved in the church. I wonder, how do you think of God?"

"Like most Christians, I suppose."

"Well, when you think about God, how do you imagine or name God?"

"Just like Jesus did."

"How's that?"

"Well, I don't know. God's all-knowing, all-loving, all-powerful, all-good."

"Is there some hymn that particularly affects you when you sing? Some way of expressing your relation to God that fits especially well for you?"

"Yes, I guess, 'How Great Thou Art.'"

They pulled out the hymnal and considered the hymn's praise to the Creator.

"The third verse is what is important to me. When I think about God sending his Son to die, I agree with the hymn writer: 'I scarce can take it in.' I'm awed that Jesus went to the cross to take away my sin."

The minister proceeded, "So your God is very great."

"Well, of course. I'm a sinner, we all are. I'd be nothing without God. I'm just a human. God is infinitely beyond my reach, but God reaches out to me. God can heal me, just as God can, well, also punish."

"So when you pray, in regard to your difficulty of not having zest, of not sleeping, how do you connect God with your problem?"

"*I ask God to take away this burden. I know in some sense I'm not worthy, but I also know God loves me.*"

"So God would have the power and perhaps the responsibility to heal you?"

"Yes."

"You have a powerful and kind God. I wonder, too, how you think of your own responsibility and power."

"I just have to accept what God gives me—burden or healing. I guess I'm not sure that I have power, or responsibility, for that matter ... except that I've come to talk with you. I guess I've taken some responsibility. I was so desperate; I finally knew I had to do something differently. I couldn't expect God to do it all."

"Let's talk about a few ways we could think about how you and God share power and responsibility. It sure makes a difference in your life whether you think of God as your Author or as a Coauthor, with you."

The Jealous God under Question

Usually the pastor did not become involved in what the children learned in Sunday school. This particular October, for some reason, it suddenly mattered a good deal to the pastor that the fourth through sixth graders memorize the Ten Commandments. Darryl, an eleven-year-old boy, took note.

"It must be pretty important. She's going to give us a quiz during the children's sermon, in front of all our parents!" he mused.

Darryl read the first two commandments: "I am the Lord your God ... you shall have no other gods before me. You shall not make for yourself an idol.... You shall not bow down to them or worship them; for I the Lord your God am a jealous God" (Exod. 20:2–5).

Darryl gathered his courage and said to his teacher, "I don't like this idea of a jealous God. I don't think God would be jealous, even of other gods."

The teacher responded, "You have a good point, Darryl. What do you think God is like?"

The Abusive, Romancing God

Sixteen-year-old Eun Hae was glad to be away from home, attending youth camp, for two reasons. First, her parents fought a lot. Though the words *domestic violence* were never spoken in her home, she had observed the cycle often enough to know viscerally what specialists explain as "the cycle of abuse." It would begin with a violent episode, then move to relief that the intense violence was over. There would follow a period of promises, remorse, flowers, and romance. Then a period of growing caution would arise, with a build-up of tensions, as fear returned with the anticipation of another episode of violence. It was like walking on thin ice, never knowing when it would break.

The other reason for Eun Hae's escape to camp was that her uncle had sexually assaulted her twice. In fact, she had signed up for this particular week of camp because she knew that her uncle would be at her home that week. He visited her family every year on his way to his annual professional meeting, and he had assaulted her at those times.

Eun Hae was not only running away from violence and assault, she was also running toward answers about God. She had made it through confirmation class without many real answers, but at that time, she had not had precise questions. Now, the two episodes with her uncle had heightened her existential theological exploration. She had also recently read the novel *Shabanu,* about a Pakistani girl who had run away rather than marry a man considerably older than herself.[7] This story prompted Eun Hae to long even more for freedom from her predicaments.

Her first night at camp, Eun Hae listened with considerable attention to the guest speaker as he preached on Hosea 2:1–13, which describes God as a dominating and abusive, yet always forgiving and romancing God. Of course, many other teens and counselors did not even notice this description of God as the passage was being read, but there it was, as clear as day to Eun Hae. She was floored! She could not believe what this preacher was saying. Was he saying *God* was like that? The preacher must be crazy … but he was reading from the *Bible*. God could *not* be like that! God could *not* be abusive!

Although usually a very private person, Eun Hae talked that night with the counselor in her cabin. She poured out explanations of some of her recent experience at home, along with her God-searching quandaries. The counselor told Eun Hae that she thought there might be times when people did *think* of God as abusive and romancing—probably when they were in pain themselves or angry with God—and that evidently the prophet Hosea was describing God in that manner to make a point to his ancient audience.[8] The counselor also pointed out that people experience God in many different ways throughout their search for meaning in their lives. But it is quite different to tell someone you *experience* God in a certain way than to suggest (or to teach others) that God is in fact *like* that. The counselor thought there were many ways to consider God, and she challenged Eun Hae to think about what she could really believe in.

IMAGINING NEW METAPHORS

We have delved into some of the creative and evocative God metaphors found in the Bible, such as Divine Potter, Shepherd, and Rock. We have met people who ran into roadblocks in their faith because of the way they imagined God, or how others presented God to them. Now we will meet some people who experienced "Eureka" moments, times when a unique metaphor for God revealed the Divine to them in a surprisingly congruent way.

I have chosen these next few examples because they illustrate breakthroughs. Two examples come from short-term groups in which participants were open to exploration, and they came up with exceptionally creative metaphors that disclosed God magnificently well for them. Two examples come from people who searched for a long while in order to imagine God in believable ways. Two are examples from my own decades-long quest for naming how I experience myself relating to the Divine. All six examples illustrate the phenomenon that occurs when someone who has been searching finds such a meaningful metaphor that he or she shouts "Yes! Oh, yes! A thousand times yes!" (And, of course, "No, not quite.")

God the Bright Night Light: A God Who Provides Comfort in the Dark

"Mom," began Jane, the mother of seven-year-old Zoë, "I don't know if you have any suggestions for us, or if I ever went through such a stage when I was a child, but we have a predicament. Zoë just is not able to go to sleep at night. She is afraid. She is not even sure of what she is afraid. Sometimes it is the possibility of a bad dream, sometimes a 'boogeyman,' sometimes a robber. Some nights she does not want to be alone. I'm going bonkers, losing my sleep as well!"

Jane listed the things they had already tried: lining up the cuddliest set of stuffed animals available, praying various prayers, singing lullabies, creating a dream catcher to hang over Zoë's head, reading soothing bedtime books (including *The Berenstain Bears and the Bad Dream*), searching closets for anything scary looking, and even discussing how the burglar alarm works. What else could they do?

The answer was not immediate. The grandmother, Jane, Zoë, and Zoë's older brother sat in the bedroom together, chatting and appreciating being there, gently seeking for clues about what to do, hoping the time together would help.

Then, during the "Word for Children" at church one Sunday, the minister mentioned various metaphors and similes for God, suggesting possibilities such as "a Caring Daddy, a Best Friend, and a Smiling Teacher."[9] When the pastor asked the children for other ways of thinking of God, Zoë screamed out, "A Bright Night Light!" Even though she had been told many times that God was always with her, Zoë needed to be able to relate to her own image of God as a Bright Night Light in order to feel secure.

God the Compass, Sail, and Wind: A God Who Helps Us Navigate

Members of a small study group were discussing how each of them thought of God. Although the participants had shared their beliefs before, they had not considered sharing useful metaphors for the Deity. Their guest facilitator encouraged them to "imagine playfully."

One couple whispered to each other, then turned to the group, explaining that they had a way of understanding God they wanted to share. To consider God, they said, they needed three images: Compass, Sail, and Wind. It turned out that they were experienced sailors. With their finite compass, their well-known sails, and the unpredictable but detectable wind, they had navigated through some difficult waters. Back on dry land, when their challenges got a bit rough, they had begun to pray, considering the Christian Trinity as the Compass, Sail, and Wind.

God the Divine Blacksmith: A God Who Knows What Fits

Another woman in that same discussion group said God was like a Divine Blacksmith. The facilitator queried, "Divine Blacksmith?" That was surely "irrelevant" as a God metaphor for this leader.

The woman explained that she had always depended on God to keep things in order. "It was as if my life, like my feet, were size 6½ B, and everything fit that size. Then my children left home for college. I felt lonely, not sure what to do. I seemed no longer to have the 'right fit' with God. I had changed, or my life had."

"So, the connection with the Divine Blacksmith … I'm not getting it," confessed the group leader. "Though I admit I know nothing about horses."

"Well, I'm just now realizing that I have been hanging on to a God that I thought would make my life neat and tidy again. I was so comfortable for so many years; now I feel lost. However, when the previous couple mentioned their Compass, Sail, and Wind God, I realized what was wrong with my picture: my view was too static. The Blacksmith makes the shoes *to fit a particular horse's feet*. I had been thinking that God should keep giving me a 6½ B shoe, but now I realize that my 'foot size' has changed. A Divine Blacksmith would give me a shoe in exactly my new size, even if I don't know what size that is."

God the Divine Physical Therapist: A God Who Helps Us Maximize Our Potential

Nancy, a woman in her late thirties, visited the church I was serving in San Diego. She had critical diabetes, which she had lived with since she was a teenager. Some of her friends believed that she needed to pray harder, to have greater faith, in order to be healed. Meanwhile, her doctor was telling her that if she did not face her limits, especially regarding her eyesight while driving a car, she could kill herself and someone else. As much as she would have liked to be healed, Nancy had a difficult time believing in what seemed like a Magic Wand God to whom she needed to keep praying harder and harder. Yet, she did believe God had some power to help her. She wondered what she believed about God, especially about what God could do with her bodily limits.

For the next four years, as we sat together before eye surgeries, visited after her leg was amputated, and laughed with joy as she learned to walk again with a prosthesis, we talked about how she might think of God. At her initiative, we considered how she might think about her power and responsibility in relation to God's. She kept searching for how to visualize God in relation to her.

One day she called me. "Carolyn, I have it: Divine Physical Therapist!" A Divine Physical Therapist, as she explained it, would know her limits and not deny them, but would also guide her to do all that was possible to make full use of her potential. She had found a metaphor for God that was authentic for her. Her human physical therapist knew her physical limits and was helping her to use what potential she had as fully as she could; wasn't that exactly what God was doing?

Nancy now was clearer about how to pray. She could pray to live as fully as possible within her current realistic limits. With the Divine Physical Therapist metaphor, she could pray for guidance, but also take responsibility for facing her limits and be open to creative ways of dealing with them. This metaphor truly bolstered and clarified her faith—and, consequently, her prayers. She explained to me that though she did not use this metaphor every time she prayed (she continued to use other metaphors, as well), the Divine Physical Therapist metaphor helped her to picture her relationship with God, especially concerning God's power.

God the Nursing Mother: A God Who Cares for Me as I Care

One of the neediest times in my life was when I was a new mother with our first child. I wrestled with how to relate to God. I had already read *Beyond God the Father*[10] and had studied about ancient goddesses. In the academic theological arena at the time, there was a healthy discourse going on about how to name God: "God/dess"? "God-S/he"?

All that discussion had been *emotionally* and *intellectually* relevant to me. Nevertheless, at this particular time, I was *physically* exhausted. When I awoke to nurse our daughter in the middle of the night, I would be groggy and wanted to feel sustained by Something Bigger than I.

All of a sudden, it was obvious to me: God was a Nursing Mother who would feed me and give me sustenance at the very same time that I held our daughter in my arms, feeding her. While my womb had held the growing fetus, I had imagined being in the Womb of God. One of myriad spiritual and therapeutic benefits of that metaphor had been the balancing of power and responsibility. I took responsibility for drinking a quart of milk a day, refraining from caffeine and alcohol, and exercising properly, but I could not be sure what was being knitted together in my womb. I had to leave that responsibility to Mother Nature, or Mother God.

Yet, it seemed that while I nursed, I had an even larger share of the responsibility. I had to eat heartily, to rest, to teach at the seminary, and to produce milk! What exactly was God doing now? Nursing Mother God became almost physical for me. She was more physical than I have ever experienced God. She was behind me, holding me up as I held my infant. Nursing Mother God seemed to be taking responsibility for me as I felt such responsibility for our daughter.

God the Uncountable Infinity: A God Who Meets My Need to Be Logical

Within the Judeo-Christian tradition, we often assume that God is infinite and human beings are finite. Though we debate and redefine our concepts of God's goodness and God's power, we do not usually question the assumption that humans are finite. However, human finitude has often been used as an excuse for too small a sense of human responsibility or ability.

Decades ago, having spent four years majoring in math in college before I decided to enter seminary, I rejoiced that both disciplines at least had infinity in common. Then I realized that theologians seemed not to know what mathematicians learn in first-year courses: there are different orders of infinity.

My religious quest met my mathematical mindset when I settled on a new way of thinking of God and humans in relation to infinity: God and humans are both infinite. God is the kind of infinity mathematicians call "uncountable," while we humans are each like a "countable" infinite set. With this new solution in my mind, I no longer needed to add a private mental disclaimer to myself when, in religious circles, I did not challenge jargon that conflicted with mathematical terminology.

I will explain what I mean, but any reader who immediately reacts to math with an "ouch" may want simply to skip to the end of this section. Don't jump over the explanation too quickly, though; it really is quite approachable and intriguing. While what follows is math, it is primarily metaphor. In fact, much of math itself is metaphor—but I leave that to mathematicians!

God could be likened to the set of all real numbers, which would include integers (1, 2, 3 ...), rational numbers (anything that can be made into a fraction), and irrational numbers (numbers like π or the square root of 3, which, no matter how hard or long you try, you can never put into a fraction).

Each human could be likened to a distinct infinite set of numbers, all of which are rational (can be made into a fraction). Multiples of 2, of 3, of ½, or 100 are all *countable infinite sets.* These sets are *countable* because it is possible to put the numbers into an array, to list them in order, and to start counting. For example: (2, 4, 6, 8 ...); (3, 6, 9, 12 ...); (½, ¼, ⅛, 1/16 ...); or (100, 200, 300, 400 ...). We cannot reach the end of these sets, for they *are* infinite. Nevertheless, these *countable* sets do have limits, created by their very definitions. A *countable infinite* set of multiples of 3, for example, will not include the number 11. Even though that set is infinite in number, it does not include all numbers.

These *countable infinite* sets describe something true, to some degree, about humans. First, we are limited beings in that we die; we do not live forever on Earth. We are also limited by circumstances, such as our size, place of birth, gender, wealth, and health. For instance, I am five feet, three inches tall, female, European American, and a twin. I could never be a professional football player or basketball player[11] and can never know what it is to be Native American. These limits are imposed upon me by my definition at birth. Like the set of multiples of 3, which does not include the number 11, I do not include certain possibilities.

However, multiples of 3, in another sense, have unending possibilities. The number 3 trillion is huge, but it can be increased immensely. In the same way, teaching, being a wife and mother, swimming, cooking, and preaching—all the things I can be and do—are things I can always be and do *better.* In fact, although I have never swum the butterfly stroke, I could learn that. I could (theoretically) learn to ice skate or to speak sign language. I could love better, have more insight, and understand more deeply. There is no limit to my potential growth in learning, doing, or being, though there are particular constraints on which things I can do and be.

Our view of humans has been too small. We are clearly defined, limited by particularity, but we are infinite. We can always incorporate more of God's infinite potential and see it in others.

We can think of God, however, as *not countable*. No matter how hard we try, we cannot put God's numbers into any array. Start at 1. If we were to try to list the next number for God's set, we could choose 1.01, but we could just as well have chosen 1.001, which is between 1 and 1.01. There is no confining God, no way to list what God contains, and no way to delineate all of God's possibilities.

Whereas humans are infinite in *range,* God, in the Uncountable Infinity metaphor, is infinite not only in range (expanding as large as any countable infinite set of numbers) but also in *density* (between any two numbers of God there are an infinite number of other numbers that can be found, and even an infinite number of numbers, like π, that cannot be found exactly).[12] Using this model, God includes all that is, but God also transcends all that is.[13] God is a different order of Being.

This metaphor for God as Uncountable Infinity and humans as countable infinite sets can help us understand a perplexity that many on religious quests encounter. "God and I are one," say those who stress unity between humans and the Divine. Others think, "Blasphemy! God transcends anything human." Persons with each view could applaud—even if they do not use the same terminology—the fact that there are *varieties of religious infinities.* Mystics could state their infinite potential and be of God, but not God. While at the same time, those, such as theologian Karl Barth, who hold to the radical difference and distance between humans and God, could be satisfied that humans and God are radically of different orders. The centuries-old debate over union or communion with the Deity could be answered by saying yes to both.

As we explore many metaphors for God, some of them will truly expand our sense of the Holy. We might feel *molded* by the Potter God, *trusting* in God the Rock, *strengthened* by the Nursing Mother God, and *secure* in the arms of a Loving Daddy.

One of the major differences in our experience of God as we use various metaphors is our sense of what God does or how God works. The Potter God *forms;* God the Compass, Sail, and Wind *guides;* and God the Bright Night Light *comforts.* We turn next to focus on what our metaphors for God reveal about our beliefs in what God can *do.*

2

God Can Do *What*?

God's Power

A SHAKY SEARCH TO UNDERSTAND GOD'S POWER

Jesus once told a parable about a mustard seed in which he said that if we have a little faith, nothing will be impossible to God (Matt. 17:20). We could interpret that to mean that God can literally move mountains or stop huge storms. Another way to view the parable is to infer that God can move myriad symbolic mountains in our lives, including our reluctant hearts, and God can help us through many stormy periods. The conversation about what kind of power God has and, therefore, what we expect from God, is a question that fills classrooms, churches, synagogues, and mosques. However, when we experience a difficult crisis, the question becomes intensely personal: "What can God do for *me*?"

No matter what our theoretical beliefs are about God's power, when life's storms hit us hard, those beliefs can get rattled. I found this out firsthand in 1994, when I happened to be near the epicenter of the Northridge, California, earthquake. I was visiting my sister's home for the weekend, before flying to Berkeley to teach a brief course. In the early morning hours of January 17, it took just three minutes, with the accompanying aftershocks, to shatter my existential theology, as well as my nerves.

There was no comparison between the Northridge quake and my childhood experiences of earthquakes while growing up in Southern California. This one was horrible. We made it from our bedrooms down the stairs, bumping on our bottoms—because the cosmos, it seemed, was too shaky for us to stand—and out onto the middle of the driveway. We sat there for several hours, most scared when a big plume of gas-fed flames erupted a few blocks away. We wondered whether to flee or to stay put. Finally, the initial emergency subsided, and by the afternoon, we cautiously reentered the house. We started picking up things, but the aftershocks continued, and we ran outside with every one. The sound of crushed glass being swept into dustpans still haunts me.

My niece arrived, like the dove with an olive branch, indicating that it was possible to navigate the roads. At my beseeching, my sister agreed that we should go to her daughter's place in Irvine for the night, but on the way, it dawned on me that I could still teach the class to which I was committed if I flew out that evening. I have never felt so relieved as when that plane took off the ground from the Orange County Airport! I was in the air, no longer having to touch Mother Earth. I felt safer to be flying—a first.

My relationship with Earth had that day become ambivalent: I would never again be able naively to enjoy hiking beautiful mountains, suntanning on beaches, or canoeing on lakes. Yet as I flew over the San Fernando Valley on the way north that evening, Earth seemed so calm and beautiful. The stars were gorgeous, just as they had been that early morning when we were sitting, terrified, on the cement driveway. Though I was out of danger, what followed was weeks and months of phone conversations during which I heard about aftershocks, details of insurance claims, and how the houses were being rebuilt.

In August of that year, I returned to California. This time, our family drove. The only way I would enter the state was with an ample water supply, a boom box, four flashlights (one for each member of the family), and four pairs of tennis shoes that were easily accessible. During an anxious week in the San Francisco Bay area, I looked for escape routes and sturdy arches at every restaurant, prayed when we traveled Bay Area Rapid Transit, listened to people discuss how they shored up their homes to render them "earthquake proof," and tried to grasp how people could carry on.

As we drove south, I witnessed the collapsed apartment building across from where my mother had lived but six months earlier, a sheered parking garage, and newly erected "sturdier" concrete-block walls that are omnipresent in Southern California.

I was terrified all over again. My family put up with my anxiety.

In my mind, I ran through Freud's list of defense mechanisms, hoping to choose one that would last for the two-week visit. *Repression* would be good, but I could not forget. *Rationalization* seemed feasible, to understand and explain. I had numerous allies, for I heard many argue, "Danger is everywhere; no reason to be more worried here." And, "The earth's already gotten readjusted here, so we're probably safer than anywhere." (These ideas sounded plausible, but did not fit with the information I had gained in the Butte, Montana, seismologist's office on the drive west. There, we had watched the computer-generated images of earthquakes that had occurred for the past forty years around the Pacific Rim. The fact was, the quakes did not occur once, then leave an area alone.)

Denial: "I am not afraid. There was no earthquake." No, that didn't work. *Projection:* "I'm not anxious, simply empathic with all these anxious people." *Introjection:* "I'll find a way to swallow the calm, the conviction that things are okay, from those around me." (Were these calm ones faithful or foolish?) But this proved too hard to chew. *Repetition compulsion.* Actually, I tried that, placing my shoes and flashlight in precisely the same spot as the night before, when we had slept safely, unawakened.

When I asked how people coped with their anxiety, the best answer I heard was, "I love my home." I could not figure out what defense that was, but it worked for the homeowner.

Leaving California that month, the state that I had loved for so many years but at that point found painful to visit, and entering Arizona, I gave a sigh of relief, slouched down in the passenger's seat of our car, and relaxed.

It was only several days later that I realized I had been searching for a God who would help me. For the first time in my life, I envied those who believed in the Almighty God that we sing about in many of our hymns. If I believed God were almighty, then I could pray that I (and my family) would be safe, or that California would have no more earthquakes. But I had passed Quake Lake, in Yellowstone; I had been reminded that all those beautiful mountains were there *because* of earthquakes and volcanoes. The metaphor of God Almighty—if we mean by "mighty" that God will stop nature's cycles and the earth's quirky behaviors—was just not all that helpful. It was difficult to conceive of an Almighty Heavenly Father reaching down to halt an earthquake. After all, earthquakes are part of what keeps our Earth living and thriving. Nature *is*. Ambiguity *is*.

I realized that the earthquake had shaken more than just the ground on which I stood. I was wrestling with bedrock questions about God, about God's power. What *can* God do? For some people, one of the casualties of disasters is the loss of faith. To expect God to be absolutely almighty, even to affect nature, can lead to huge disappointment in God. Other people come to a deeper faith in the midst of a disaster. Almost all of us realize at a time of crisis that we need a faith check.

What *do* we believe?

AN ATTITUDE OF INQUIRY

The book of Job is a drama that inquires into suffering—specifically, what is the cause of suffering? It begins, "There was once a man in the land of Uz whose name was Job" (Job 1:1). Job is every man, every woman—a character with whom many of us can identify.

This story is not a monologue. Job is on stage with others—his so-called friends—who give their opinions about why he is suffering. On stage as well are God and a being that is translated "Satan," but more true to the original Hebrew would be "the satan."[1]

At the outset of the drama, it is assumed that God is in control of the earth. When God presses Job with the question, "Who makes the lightning?" the obvious answer is God. Job, too, assumes that God is in control.

It is also assumed that human suffering is the result of disobeying God. That is what Job's "friends" keep insisting: "Surely you've done something wrong, since you have all this suffering." (Not much has changed in this regard; many people who suffer today find out that others think anyone who suffers must have done something wrong.)

The twist in this biblical drama is that Job knows better. He knows that some people suffer even when they do not deserve punishment, that people like himself have done nothing wrong. This is where the book of Job gets really interesting. The narrative entertains the idea that perhaps suffering occurs *without a cause that we can understand.*

The choir at the Orange County church that I served sings a resounding arrangement of a piece titled "Beyond Our Understanding." When I approach questions of massive suffering, I sometimes wish I could join the choir just to sing that anthem boldly. In many ways, this anthem sums up the message of Job: the key to suffering lies "beyond our understanding" (Job 36:26).

Yet "beyond our understanding" does not mean "beyond our inquiry."

The Wisdom Literature of the Hebrew Bible (which includes not only the book of Job, but also the Psalms, Proverbs, Ecclesiastes, and the Song of Solomon) is written with an *attitude of inquiry.*[2] It is with that same attitude that I approach the question of what God can *do* in relation to natural disasters, such as the Northridge earthquake. Tsunamis, hurricanes, cyclones, and collapsing bridges and mines raise the same query for millions of people: what is God doing? These are horrible, horrendous events.

When we wonder about the connection between earthquakes, tsunamis, cyclones, and God, we are really questioning the relationship among God, the earth (or nature), and suffering. What happens between God and the earth? Can God intervene in the earth's behavior?

The earth is gorgeous and kind. But we also know that its forces can kill us. Why nature includes suffering is left beyond our understanding. Suffering occurs—human suffering and the suffering of other creatures. (I want to make an important distinction here: suffering is not the same as evil. My attitude of inquiry leads me to believe that the earth does not do evil; it *intends* no harm. The earth's forces just are. Forces of nature lead to horrible consequences that make for immense amounts of *suffering,* but the earth's forces are not evil.)

While the relationship between God and Earth may be beyond our understanding, we do have a relationship with God *and* with Earth. We do tend to believe that God cares for us and, presumably, also for the earth. The first creation story in Genesis (1:1–2:4a) repeats again and again, "It is good," referring to creation. Yet when horrendous natural disasters occur, as with the Indian Ocean tsunami of 2004, Hurricane Katrina in 2005, the Myanmar cyclone and China earthquakes in 2008, or one of the worst natural disasters since the fifteenth century—the 1974 famine in Ethiopia—we naturally wonder about nature or God's goodness.

What causes what? What can we depend on? Where is God's care evident? Some people survive devastating tsunamis, hurricanes, cyclones, and earthquakes. Certainly, God was caring for them. But God cared no less for those who did not survive. Besides caring, I believe God also mourns. Perhaps Earth does, too.

In ancient times, humans were so dependent on the earth that they often thought of Earth itself as God, or Goddess. It was the forces of nature with which they sought to live in harmony, or tried to placate. Just as the Bible presents different views of God and God's relation to the world, so do people who believe in God today have several opinions about how God relates to the suffering caused by natural disasters:

1. Natural disasters are acts of God. For whatever reason, God causes them.
2. Nature is neutral; God cares. God cannot hold back a tidal wave, but God cares.
3. God has the power to affect, even control nature, but God chooses not to intervene.

If we take the first position and think that God, in some sense, *causes* natural disasters, or the third position, that God *chooses* not to intervene, then we might as well step onto the stage with Job and ask God for some explanation. Surely, we might argue, out of the tens of thousands of people who die in tsunamis, cyclones, and hurricanes, there must be *some* very good people who are worth saving.

Maybe God created the world the way it is—beautiful, yet incredibly complex—and it still has a few flaws. (If I had my preference, God would have made human knees a little better!) Maybe God is working on it.

One thing I learned about asking questions is that we can miss something if we stay focused on only one part of a picture.

If we are considering God, the earth, and suffering, perhaps we can learn something about *God* by considering the *earth*.

Before experiencing the Northridge earthquake, I, like many humans, took the earth for granted. The earth was an "it." A nice "it," a beautiful one. But an "it" that I used. I never gave any thought to the earth as having a living, dynamic existence of its own. I had never before considered being angry with the earth. Yet as I realized that I was actually in relation it, I also valued it more. I could no longer solely use the earth in a selfish way, for my needs alone. I plant a seed and the earth grows it; I walk and the wind blows my hair. I began to think of Earth as having a life of its own with which I needed to cooperate. For the ongoing life of the planet, earthquakes and tidal waves will happen.

While I might personally wish that God could hold back a tidal wave and stop gravity for a few minutes at times, it seems that nature's forces continue. Yet I fully believe that God is there, helping as much as God can. That is what happened in the book of Job: God appeared and was with Job. Even though God never answered Job's questions, God was *with* Job. While it may not be in God's nature to stop earthquakes or storms, we can trust that God is trying desperately to help us find safety and to help each other—before, during, and after such disasters.

I believe God *does* help us to put all this chaos and uncertainty into perspective as we maintain our faith in a loving and caring life. We can respond wisely in our building on the earth; we can diminish our chances of being involved in a natural disaster by living away from faults and coastlines—yet those are often magnificently beautiful places where thousands choose to live or have to live. Then, certainly, we can choose to take responsible precautions and to make structural changes in how we live on the land.

After the Northridge earthquake, I realized that if we had been in tepees on January 17, there would have been little danger. The earth rarely opens up such that people fall through; our houses fall upon us. We do know safer ways to build than we implement. "Please, God," I thought, "be more effective in persuading us to follow your ways."

I preferred never to go west of the California Aqueduct again, but I had family there. Several years later, I moved back! I do not want life to be ambiguous, but it is. No God can guarantee that life is not. We cannot prepare for many unknowns in nature; there are genuine dangers and risks inherent in life on Earth. We can choose our commitments and face our anxieties (using defense mechanisms if we need to); we can, sometimes, choose to be calm and to see beauty. Life requires us to live with courage in the midst of a loving community.

I wish life were completely orderly. If we did such-and-such, this or that would happen. Do good; only good will happen to us. That may be true to some degree, but there is a lot in our universe, on our Earth, and in our personal lives that is "beyond our understanding" (Job 36:26).

With an attitude of inquiry, we may consider that God seeks consistently to do what was named in the creation story: to create good out of chaos. We might conceptualize God as a Choreographer of Chaos.[3] God takes what is and helps it to become what it can be. Even while a tsunami wave is forming, God probably begins the choreography: encouraging people to notice strange things, to run, to carry others, to hang on to palm trees, to climb stairs. Even while a plate of the earth is shifting, God probably begins to nudge people to be attentive, to go under cover. I can imagine God choreographing the massive relief work that is to come, even our part in that. God may be choreographing right now research into how we can spare lives in the midst of natural disasters.

Earth is wonderful, and we can have a marvelous relationship with it—even if that includes anger at times. My particular inquiry maintains the attitude that God is caring, always caring, and always Choreographing the Chaos so that we might dance—together.

A HUNDRED WAYS OF WONDERING

You probably have heard the expression "Jumping Jehoshaphat!" Though the origin of the phrase is not exactly clear, it likely refers to the behavior of an interesting and passionate leader in ancient days. The story told in the Hebrew Bible is of a huge crisis facing King Jehoshaphat's people: a great army was approaching, and they were on the verge of war. The king mobilized all the people, requiring absolutely everyone to be involved. Creatively, he mobilized them for worship, in order *not* to have to mobilize them for war. When they were gathered, Jehoshaphat did three things. First, he recollected all the *good things* God had done for them. Then, he named all the *good reasons* the people should be confident in God at that time. Finally, Jehoshaphat described the current human predicament, asking God to intervene. At one point Jehoshaphat said to God, quite honestly, "We are powerless against this great multitude that is coming against us. We do not know what to do, but our eyes are on you" (2 Chron. 20:12).

The result? War was averted! Can't you just see the leader and people jumping for joy? There was peace instead of war. The phrase "Jumping Jehoshaphat" aptly captures our relief when a graceful solution emerges from a crisis.

Whether we are mobilizing for war, have been through a natural disaster, or are stunned in the wake of a collapsing coal mine or a falling bridge, many of us, like Jehoshaphat, cry to God in our distress: we don't know what to do! Are we as confident as Jehoshaphat when we ask God to intervene?

Thornton Wilder, in his Pulitzer prize–winning novel *The Bridge of San Luis Rey,* raises the question of why terrible things happen to "innocent" people. The story starts out, "On Friday noon, July the twentieth, 1714, the finest bridge in all Peru broke and precipitated five travelers into the gulf below."[4] It was just a little bridge, handmade more than a century earlier by Incas (the Native Americans of Peru), but in the people's minds, "the bridge seemed to be among the things that last forever; it was unthinkable that it should break."[5] The bridge breaking, and the death of the five people who were walking on it, rattled the whole area of Lima, Peru.

The storyteller ponders: "It was rather strange that this event should have so impressed the Limeans, for in that country those catastrophes which lawyers shockingly call the 'acts of God' were more than usually frequent.... That is why it was so surprising that the Peruvians should have been especially touched by the rent in the bridge of San Luis Rey."[6]

The story goes on to tell of a certain priest, Brother Juniper, who witnessed the accident and decided that he had a perfect laboratory to prove that God is in complete control of our lives, that God willed the death of exactly those five people. Brother Juniper spent years researching the lives of these five, even making statistical charts, comparing the victims, using the categories of "goodness," "piety," and "usefulness."[7]

Though Brother Juniper wrote a huge book about all his research, he ended up quite discouraged, because, quite truthfully, his conclusion was this: "The discrepancy between faith and the facts is greater than is generally assumed."[8] When he tried to make some sense of his discovery, he found that there was no sense to be made of those particular five people dying. Yet, in order to maintain his view that God wills what happens, Brother Juniper decided that this bridge accident did two things: one, it punished a few bad people with death; and, two, it rewarded a few good people with death, that is, an early call to heaven.

Though we might scoff at Brother Juniper's conclusions that disregard the evidence, if we are honest, his questions and answers are not that different from ours when we are desperate to make sense of things. Are his conclusions our only alternatives? Either human life is under the total control of God or God does not exist (or is indifferent)?

Thornton Wilder tucks one sentence into his little book that gives us a clue to another perspective: *"There are a hundred ways of wondering at circumstance."*[9]

People are different. Some of us are so proud of our abilities that we pretend to be certain of things about which, really, we are not so sure. Others of us will act only after we do much research and take plenty of precautionary measures. Then, we still blame ourselves—or God—if there is an accident. Others take life more as it comes, neither seeking certainty nor worrying about uncertainty.

I remember a time when my family went to Ensenada, Mexico, to immerse ourselves in Spanish. We were standing in the kitchen of our host family when the father and one son said something in Spanish our family did not understand, so they explained the phrase to us.

Their words, *"Ojalá te vaya bien,"* were an expression often said in Mexico that means, "God willing," or something like, "I hope." Another phrase they often used was, *"Si Dios quiere,"* which they translated as, "God decides." Literally, it means, "If God wants."

"We can never be certain things will go well," they explained. Their phrases expressed a slight reluctance in regard to certainty, a kind of humility before an uncertain life. Their uncertainty generated a mood of openness to Wisdom.

"Jumping Jehoshaphat" is the mood that King Jehoshaphat generated when he sought the power of God. Jehoshaphat had a frame of mind that is relevant for all time—and for political as well as religious leaders. He had an honest humility about what he knew and did not know. He admitted, "We do not know what to do, but our eyes are on you" (2 Chron. 20:12), thereby seemingly creating room to learn what could be learned. With this attitude—before we build bridges, before we dig mines, before we go to war—we may be most open to the Wisdom of the Divine and humble before the forces of nature.

In ancient Hebrew days, Wisdom was thought to be a divine companion to God. There have also been many throughout the centuries who have likened Jesus to God's Wisdom on earth. The Wisdom of God, unfortunately, is not sent out over the airwaves or shouted from a divine megaphone—getting our attention so that we can choose to follow it or not. However, our very stopping to ask for Divine Wisdom, as Jehoshaphat did, might help us to be humble in important endeavors. We are more likely to pick up knowledge if we admit that we need it.

When we are open, the persuasive Wisdom of the universe seems to empower us to sense something more, a bigger picture, a greater range of options. While we do not have to conclude that God is in complete control, neither do we have to take on the whole responsibility ourselves.

POWERFUL OPTIONS

My basic premise throughout this book is that our metaphors for God are not of little concern. When there is a crisis—a cyclone, an earthquake, or a car accident—it is a serious issue whether we believe God can or cannot intervene. If we visualize God as a Potter, Puppeteer, or Lord, the implication may be that God will step in and do something about the situation. If God, then, does not intervene, we may experience a crisis of faith. On the other hand, if people are spared, we may credit God with a miracle. There are many ways to envision God's power, and the metaphors we use and with which we are comfortable often suggest what we think about God's power. When we see what the metaphors we use actually suggest about God's power, sometimes we realize we need a different metaphor.

Go back, for a moment, to the individuals introduced in the first section of this book. It is very telling that when these people found unique metaphors for God that became meaningful for them, they tended to alter how they imagined God's power, and that shift became evident in their vital God metaphor. For example, George began with a "How Great Thou Art" metaphor for God that implicitly put the power entirely in God's hands. After talking things over with his pastor, George acknowledged his own power to make some things happen and claimed more of that power by entertaining the idea of God as Coauthor, rather than Author. This gave him a way of thinking about God that matched his life experience—that both God and he affected what happened to him. This shift helped him to take more responsibility without losing his belief in a present and plenty-enough-powerful Deity.

Nancy's metaphor for God as the Divine Physical Therapist was long sought after. She had been actively looking for a metaphor that would reflect her genuine belief in the delicate balance of power and responsibility that God and she shared in the course of her living with diabetes. Naming God as Divine Physical Therapist was a theological breakthrough for her that contributed to congruence between her belief and her behavior.

Similarly, the image of a Divine Blacksmith, who makes shoes to fit, reflected the belief and experience of the woman who faced a new loneliness in her life after her children had left home.

For the exhausted husband whose wife had been ill for two years, the intentional shift from Lord to Love allowed him to rest from his plea for instant healing and opened up the possibility of a wider angle of sight with regard to what God's healing might include.

Even little Zoë, who came up with the metaphor of God as a Bright Night Light, found an image of God's power that helped her through her particular youthful struggle.

Consider someone who has power in your life. How do they affect you? How do they get you to do something? To *not* do something? In human relations it is true that some "power" comes from a kind of force: "Do this, or else." "Do not do that, or else." But consider someone who has power in your life and does not use any kind of coercion. It is probable that this person uses the power of love.

Love can carry enormous power. If someone loves another and is loved in return, all the lover needs to do is nod with a smile, and the other is empowered to proceed. The lover frowns, and the other stops short, checking his or her behavior. The parent hugs, and the child is empowered. The parent seems disturbed, and the child wonders about approval. A splendid boss who cares deeply about workers may empower workers to love their jobs and to enjoy the community atmosphere of the workplace. Love is amazingly powerful. What do you think: Is it *all*-powerful? Or would you describe it as very persuasively powerful?

Think of situations where a person uses coercive power—where one person makes something happen. The boss fires someone without communal reflection. The teacher will not listen to the explanations of the usually attentive students and instead says, "Sit down in your seat." The coach does not want any "excuses" and benches latecomers without discussion. What kind of actual power do these coercive people have? Yes, they get their way, but do the employees, students, and team members care as much? Are they empowered to perform better, or are they left feeling unheard, unwanted, unimportant? Are these recipients of all-power actually empowered as fully as they would be if they were recipients of persuasive love?

Much hinges upon our internalized notions of what *all-powerful* means. Does it mean the ability to make something happen, or does it mean caring relentlessly within the community?

As you consider the range and ramification of God's power in each of the descriptions below, ask yourself: "What do I *really* believe about God's power?" These options are certainly not the only possible scenarios, but they show a wide range of possibilities. Most likely, you will hold a mixture of these positions. As you read, let yourself take a playful "Jumping Jehoshaphat" stance. Maybe something new will leap out at you!

Total Power: God, the Almighty

"Praise to the Lord, the Almighty, the King of creation!" How many of us have sung the words to this hymn without thinking what we actually mean by the term *Almighty*? For some, an Almighty God implies a Magic Wand God. While that phrase may seem pejorative, it describes the kind of power many expect from God—that God can wave a wand to stop an earthquake or tidal wave. The metaphor of God as Genie[10] conveys a similar expectation—that we can rub the vase, pray, and expect that whatever we desire will occur. From this vantage point, God can make everything happen. When there is a personal or communal crisis, millions of Christians and Jews have a knee-jerk reaction: they think of God as somehow making (or allowing) the crisis to happen, sometimes persuading themselves that the apparent bad is really good in disguise.

Trying to explain an all-mighty God as all-good and all-powerful *and* to explain the existence of bad or evil in the world at the same time poses a conundrum. Many in the Judeo-Christian tradition discover, to their surprise, that when push comes to shove, they do not actually believe in the existence of evil because they conclude that God is all-good *and* all-powerful (*power* meaning, for them, "the ability to make happen"). The logical conclusion of this view is that, since God *is* good, God would not do anything bad to God's creatures. Since God is in control and all-powerful, God's will *is* what *does* happen in the world.

Yet, when we consider devastating war, holocausts, massive oppression, and poverty alongside ease and luxury, it is difficult to hold to this position, or to hold to a metaphor of God that is all-powerful—if that power is considered to be the capacity to do what God wants.

Still, for many, this Almighty God is the most relevant metaphor for God. Some manage to maintain this thinking by defining areas in which this power is not applicable—over nature, for example.

In truth, we do not usually name forthrightly the kind of power God has. We do not say, "God who is able to make whatever God wants to happen by forcing it to be so." Neither do we say, "God who persuades us through guidance found in our dreams, body wisdom, rational thinking, scripture, friendships, beauty, and community discernment." Most often, we simply assume that God should somehow be all-powerful. Yet, that "all" could refer to different kinds of power.

For example, preacher Henry Mitchell explains that all-powerful within many African American contexts is not the all-powerful-to-make-happen God that it is in the minds of many European Americans. The African-influenced idea of "all-powerful" is more communal, more reflective of the ancient Hebrew tradition where the Sovereign entered into covenants with people.[11]

I once participated in a Doctor of Ministry seminary group where several African American clergywomen described how they used variations of Almighty Heavenly Father and Lord as metaphors for God in their women's healing groups. Even though these metaphors suggest the absolute power of God, the women told me that they were not trying to convey the absolute power of God in an exclusive sense. They explained how there can be deep *healing* with God who is spoken of as all-powerful to help in difficult situations, without the implication that God *created* the difficult situations. These women taught me that believing God to be all-powerful was precisely what would motivate some people to take enormous responsibility for themselves in the midst of trouble. Within this African American context, this all-powerful God was able to evoke shared responsibility and hope without blaming God for the problems.

Every denomination's hymnal includes nuanced and intermixed views of God. To say God is Almighty could mean that

God makes something happen (as in the hymn "God Will Take Care of You") or that God loves with persuasive strength (as in the hymn "O God Who Shaped Creation").

One person can sing, "Praise to the Lord, the Almighty, the King of Creation," and be thinking of the Magic Wand God because that is the way he or she thinks of Lord or King. Others who sing the same words may be thinking quite differently. This hymn itself—with its lofty, all-powerful images in the title—includes metaphors that suggest other types of power, such as the power of protection and sheltering us under gentle wings. Those who are singing seldom realize that they are naming metaphors for God that imply drastically different types of divine power.

Metaphors such as Puppeteer, Author, and Potter all convey a similar sense of God as being "the one in charge," an almighty power who makes things happen. Yet even these metaphors have nuances that hint at other possibilities. Those who are most knowledgeable about the professions of puppetry, writing, and pottery making have playfully shared with me that what at first seems all-powerful is, upon intimate experience, not so totally in the control of the one expected to be in charge. I was told by a couple of puppeteers that some puppets have a "mind of their own." Fictional characters do not always bend to their author's intent. Neither does clay always cooperate with the potter. Pueblo storytellers say that they work with clay until the clay "speaks" or until there is attunement with the clay. With this understanding of the responsiveness between clay and potter, the metaphor of God as Potter would not suggest that God has complete power. If clay "speaks," God does not so much "make" a pot, as work with the responsiveness of the clay.

There are many metaphors for God that do *not* suggest that God is Almighty. These next options tend more to foster the idea of human responsibility and freedom in relation to God's will.

Restrained Power: God the Post-heroic CEO, God the Tough Love Parent

Some who hold the conviction that God is almighty deal with the implication that humans, then, do not have genuine freedom by concluding that God sometimes *chooses* to restrain God's own power. God chooses *not* to act, in order to "allow" humans to have real freedom.

During my two decades as a seminary professor, I witnessed numerous students who arrived with an image of an Almighty God. They wrestled with the question, "If God is All-Powerful, how could humans still have freedom to act, and sometimes do horrible things?" They struggled with the three statements that are difficult to explain at the same time: God is all-powerful; God is good; there is evil in the world. They studied numerous possible responses to this conundrum, and many students shifted to a view that God is Almighty, but "allows" humans to have freedom.

I find this position the least satisfying of all options, for if I were to believe that God has the power to save people from a crisis, but *chooses not to*—even for the laudable intent to permit human freedom—I would be inconsolably angry at God! However, this position is extremely attractive to some, for it preserves God's absolute mightiness, but admits that humans are free to make wise or unhealthy choices.

Two metaphors drawn from human relations convey the kind of power God is expected to have in this theological position. One comes from language used in the business world; the other borrows psychological jargon for parenting.

In the business world, the concept of a post-heroic CEO emerged to describe a new style of management, a shift from the "heroic" managers of the past who made all the decisions to CEOs who distribute power to others, for the sake of a more productive company. The idea is that the post-heroic CEO hands over decision making and responsibility to several leaders within the company, trusting and encouraging those with the newly given power. The CEO is still in charge of the business, and everyone in the company knows that the CEO is *able* to take charge at any time. However, the CEO intends not to intercede, but to stand beside and to empower. If there is a crisis, the workers might *want* the CEO to step in to fix things. Will the post-heroic CEO do that? While the old-fashioned heroic CEO (in theory) would ride in on a horse to solve all of the problems, the post-heroic CEO (in theory) has reorganized the business relationships so that the employees—as well as the business—experience the consequence of their own actions.

The metaphor of God as Post-heroic CEO conveys the concept of God being all-powerful (to make things happen), but allowing human freedom. From this position, while God *could* intervene, God usually does not, preferring to maintain the promise to grant self-determination.

Another metaphorical way of looking at the same view is to think of God as a Tough Love Parent. The result is the same as the Post-heroic CEO, but the context is familial, not business oriented. This Tough Love Parent God knows that the child must learn responsibility, and so declares precise rules. The Tough Love Parent will not rescue the child. If the child goofs up, the child suffers the consequences; that is, the child is responsible. However, the Tough Love Parent will always be there, loving, accepting, and naming responsible behavior.

While at first glance this metaphor seems like an attractive way to think of God's power, the Tough Love stance may become disturbing to us when times get really rough. We may end up imagining God as "holding God's hands behind God's back," and wonder why God doesn't offer us more help. With both the Post-heroic CEO and the Tough Love Parent images of God, we might reasonably ask, "What's the point of God having that power? If God can intervene, but doesn't, isn't that cruel?"

The Power of Presence: God with Us

When I listen to people praying, I realize that many want, above all, to think of God as *with* them. People pray for friends and family who are traveling, asking that "God be with them." When they pray for those with health concerns, the request is the same: "God be with them." Congregations pray, "God be with us." The power of God that is most crucial for them is the *power of presence*.

Many Christians think of Jesus as God-with-us. Decades ago, Episcopal priest and author Malcolm Boyd made famous the phrase *"Are you running with me, Jesus?"*[12] His book by that name was a marvelous account of daily dialogues with the Divine-in-the-midst of life, *with* us. Precisely because Jesus lived, breathed, and worked on behalf of those considered the least, he was able to understand their daily living, working, suffering, and searching. In a sense, Jesus becomes a divine metaphor, a way of thinking of God-with-us, walking beside us.

One pastor I know uses Shekinah as her dominant metaphor for God. This Hebrew word means "hovering presence." By using a less familiar way of naming God and capitalizing on the sense of God-with-us, the pastor seeks to re-engage women who have left churches because they did not feel included when God was referred to exclusively in male terms.

I recently discovered a fascinating contemporary metaphor that connotes, as Shekinah does, a "hovering presence." However, at first I was not so sure I liked the implications of the metaphor, when potentially applied to God.

More than two decades ago, when our children were three or four years old, they moved from half-day preschool to full-day preschool, which meant that they carried their lunch to school—or, rather, we drove them to school, along with their lunch. One day I took our daughter to school, but she did not have her lunch, so I dashed home to get it, then brought it back.

The director of the school greeted me at the front door of the building as I arrived with the forgotten lunch in hand. She said to me, "So, will you be bringing your daughter her lunch if she forgets it when she is in college?" I was taken aback. College? That sounded like a long time off to me. This was a Montessori preschool, and the philosophy, which I tend to like, is that people need to be responsible for themselves. The director pointed out that if Alexandra did not have any lunch *that* day, she would remember her lunch in the future. True, I thought, as I ignored the director and walked to our daughter's classroom to hand her the lunch, with a smile on my face.

I do not know what the director would have called a parent who brought their daughter a forgotten lunch in college, but today there is a name for that kind of parent—"helicopter parent." Helicopter parents hover closely overhead and watch out for their children, whether or not the children need them. It is a pejorative term; it suggests that the parents are overprotective or overcontrolling of their children, especially their children's education. I guess staff at colleges use this term to refer to the parents who call frequently about their children.

When I heard that term for parents, given my propensity to think about ways of imagining God, I immediately wondered whether considering God as a Helicopter God would be positive or pejorative. That is, is it positive or not to consider God as hovering over us, sometimes creating a lot of wind around a circumstance to get our attention? Is it positive or pejorative to consider God somehow providing for us what we need, even what we have forgotten? Whether or not it is positive, is it *true*? Is God like a helicopter parent?

In one sense, I think God is our Helicopter God, in that God does come into all sorts of circumstances, swooping into places it seems no one could go to help. I do believe that God hovers over us, is a presence that reaches us.

However, in the jargon used regarding parenting today, God is not a Black Hawk helicopter! Parents who cross the line from merely having a good deal of zeal in their parenting into what is unethical behavior, such as writing their children's college admission essays, are called "Black Hawks" because those military helicopters are very powerful and have huge capabilities.

When parents are compared to intrusive helicopters, it is because they have crossed an ethical line regarding what a parent should do. Theologically, we can say that God cannot be a Black Hawk helicopter because God simply cannot live our lives for us. God can *be there* for us, but cannot solve everything. In huge crises such as cyclones, hurricanes, and earthquakes, surely God hovers over all people, but God cannot just drop energy biscuits and life preservers from the sky to feed and rescue the thousands of people stranded by these catastrophes. I trust that our Helicopter God stirs up the leaders of nations and the United Nations and nudges the hearts and minds of creative, caring people everywhere to solve these massive problems. Even though God may hover, God needs humans to cooperate, just as parents and their children cooperate.

The Power of Pure Being: God *Is*

Plenty of people in the Judeo-Christian tradition want God to be personal, so they attribute personhood or personality to the Deity. As I have mentioned before, there are strands in the Bible that talk of God as even physically "walking" on earth. However, there are other passages where the abstractness of God is lifted up. God is Spirit, Breath.

Sometimes thinking of God being like anything remotely human is frustrating. We might say, "God is *like* an author," but if we know an author, we might have difficulty figuring out how

God is like that person in any way! We might wish for a metaphor that is not complicated by our projection of human attributes onto God.

When Zoë needed God to be there with her through the night and came up with the metaphor Bright Night Light, her metaphor was not personal in the sense of having a personality. Bright Night Light is not anthropomorphic. Yet, this way of imagining God provided her with comfort, "light." It made her feel a sense of the presence of God.

There are many metaphors for God that point to God in the abstract, a Divine Presence that just *Is:* Music Itself, Directing Creativity, Spiritual Presence, Ground of Being,[13] and the Source of Creative Good.[14] My experience is that people who most consistently think of God in these "pure being" terms consider themselves to have a great deal of responsibility. God provides Directing Creativity, but it is up to them to receive what God offers and to use it wisely. If they are ill, they are less likely to blame God, or to think that it is "God's will" for them to be ill.

Abstract qualities, such as creativity and justice, can be impersonal, just as gravity is. Yet, however impersonal gravity is because of its universal nature—it holds *everyone* to the earth—it is also quite personal, because gravity holds *me* down. In this way, what seems to be an impersonal God that is imagined with abstract qualities becomes personally relevant. Nevertheless, those who prefer a personal God, meaning that they visualize a Being, may have difficulty *experiencing* these abstract ways of conceiving of God.

The Power of Good Intentions: Ambiguous God

Jungian psychologists propose that we tend to reach the age of about thirty-five before we integrate our various polarities. If we are primarily introverted, for example, by thirty-five, we have become aware of our ability to be extroverted as well. If we have perceived ourselves as becoming angry easily, by then we may realize that we can also be amazingly tolerant and patient in circumstances that might evoke anger. We may be assertive, but we can also be passive; passive, yet also assertive. By thirty-five, if we are honest with ourselves, we see ourselves with some hues of gray (not just in hair color). By this early middle age, we can begin to face the ambiguity that is inherent in all of life: there is good and bad in all, including ourselves; life and death are close together; that of which we are most sure, we can also doubt; what we think makes us secure also binds us.

As I considered how this acceptance of ambiguity might apply to God, I made up a silly metaphor that I cannot imagine anyone ever using, but it captures one concept of God that people have: God the Caregiver over Thirty-Five Accepting Her/His Own Ambiguity. Some people who are fed up with a God who is described as perfect, all-knowing, and all-loving, or a God who seems to "allow" or cause harm, *find* God in a new and creative way when they are able to think of God as filled with ambiguity, too. From this viewpoint, God is trying hard, is aiming toward good for us, but God is not perfect.

While this image of God may seem far-fetched, it is actually a position found in one strand of the Hebrew Bible. The strand of writing that speaks of God as Yahweh reveals an ambiguously good God. God wrestles with God's self, consults others, seeks to do good, but can and does threaten and destroy.

Remember Darryl, the boy I described who was troubled in Sunday school with the idea of a jealous God? Or Eun Hae, the young woman at youth camp who was appalled by the Abusive and Romancing Husband metaphor for God found in Hosea 2:1–13, Jeremiah 2:1–3, 13:20–27, and Ezekiel 16:24? While these metaphors are extreme examples of ambiguity, the scriptures do describe God at times as not "all good." Even as God tries to do good overall, many stories suggest that God has a potential mean streak, that God can be jealous, even destructive.

Clearly, this way of thinking of God is unthinkable for many who require God, at bare minimum, to be all good. Yet it is important to recall that metaphors are helpful *only* if they evoke both the reaction, "God is like that," and the response, "God is *not* like that!" For some, God can be *experienced* as a jealous God, even an Abusive Husband, but also *not be* like that. The Caregiver over Thirty-Five Accepting Her/His Own Ambiguity is a metaphor that includes ambiguity without *intentional* "meanness." For those who have lived with so much bad or horror, or who are especially attuned to ambiguity in all of life, this way of thinking of God helps them believe in God—who is ambiguous, just like they are!

As a part of their healing, survivors *and* perpetrators of violence are often encouraged to come to terms with their ambiguity, their capacity to do good as well as evil, evil as well as good.[15] They also need to see this ambiguity in others, so that they can have appropriate trust and mistrust in others. It is not necessarily helpful to think, "I won't get into a relationship with a bad partner again," for "bad" and "good" come in the same human being; the same person is sometimes one, sometimes the other. Fully owning our own capacities for a range of feelings and behaviors helps us to see that potential in others and to be attuned to healthy dynamics in relationships. Facing ambiguity helps us be wary of anything "too good to be true," and at the same time to have wisdom and compassion for the "mean streak" in many.

The other part of the metaphor, God as Caregiver, is important. Caregivers do good; while they may be edgy, short-sighted, or impatient some days, they want the best for those they genuinely care about. Caregivers are usually patient, knowing that humans are complex. Caregivers sometimes unintentionally do something that seems mean, or is mean to the one they care for. They may make an unreasonable demand, place an unrealistic limit, or insult someone for whom they are caring. Caregivers are not perfect; they are ambiguous, aiming toward good.

Caregivers who are in touch with their own ambiguity are wise in caring for others. Caregivers who counsel or teach or parent can tolerate uncertainty, will not be duped by insistent promises that are not kept, and will hang in there with what is. *Because* they are caregivers, they aim in the direction of more shalom, more wholeness, more responsibility.

The greatest asset of this metaphor for God is that some people who cannot imagine a perfect Being, given such an imperfect world, may find spiritual satisfaction as they visualize a Presence that is, in fact, imperfect—that is, ambiguous. Whether or not creatures are considered to be more good than bad, God is at least considered exceptionally desirous of good, overall. God *intends* good, always.

The Power of Love: God as Dynamic Love

I want to go back to Thornton Wilder's *The Bridge of San Luis Rey* for a moment. After the collapse of the bridge and the death of "innocent" people, Brother Juniper wanted to prove that God was in complete control. However Brother Juniper did not have the last word. The abbess at the orphanage, who had cared for two children who died on the bridge, did not try to convince anyone of anything. She simply had "thoughts passing in the back of her mind": "Soon we shall die and all memory of those five will have left the earth, and we ourselves shall be loved for a while and forgotten. But the love will have been enough; all those impulses of love return to the love that made them. Even memory is not necessary for love. There is a land of the living and a land of the dead and the bridge is love, the only survival, the only meaning."[16]

The abbess did not try to figure out what kind of power God had, or how God was involved in the accident. She simply had, in the back of her mind, thoughts that named her experience: *memories fade, but love lasts.*

The abbess's response suggests one of the answers to the question of God in relation to crises: *God offers the power of Dynamic Love, period*. This metaphor for God, Dynamic Love, empowers us to see God at work in situations and also to recognize our own responsibility. There is uncertainty and risk in life. If a rope on a bridge is weak, it will break, no matter how good or bad the people are who are walking on that bridge. If the rifle of a soldier in war shoots a precious child, no matter how loved and good the child is, and no matter what side of the war the soldier is on, the child is killed. But God is still the power of Dynamic Love, and God keeps showing love to us, patiently, tenderly, forever, at all times. Sensing Infinite Love helps us to make meaning and to find wonder in the life that we have not yet figured out.

When our son, Stephen, died, one of my biggest fears was that I would lose some memories of him. At first I worked tenaciously to remember, to hold on to remembering. A year laer, my experience matched the abbess's "thoughts passing in the back of the mind"[17]: love is a bridge, what survives, what has meaning. Of course I regret deeply that we do not have current events to share as a family with Stephen, but I no longer feel that I have to hold tightly to memories. Love is enough.

For me, it is enough for God to be and to have the power of Dynamic Love. Instead of thinking of God's power as similar to the physical force of the moon's pull on the tides or the power of a command or a thunderbolt, I find it more helpful to consider God's power as consistent, dependable Love. I have come to see God's Love not only as important, but also as sufficient.

The Power of Transformation: God as Persistent Life

Many years ago, when our daughter was in second grade, she had an assignment to find a caterpillar. That seemed a difficult task, but lo and behold, we found two while biking on a gorgeous path that always reminded me of a Louisiana Bayou, even though it was along a river in Dayton, Ohio. We put each caterpillar in a jar with twigs, grass, and water. This occurred in October. Alexandra took one jar to school, to stay in the classroom, and we put the other on top of our refrigerator at home. To my surprise, the caterpillar did indeed cuddle up to the twig and turn into a cocoon. Then, nothing happened.

The caterpillar that went to school also turned into a cocoon, and nothing happened.

Early in February, the second-grade teacher threw away the dead cocoon, but we were not so tidy at home, forgetting about the jar amid the refrigerator clutter. Then, on exactly the first day of spring, something moving caught my attention. Things actually worked as they were supposed to! A butterfly emerged! We took it outside where it flew away, presumably happy.

We speak about life, death, and resurrection. We experience the life and the death of loved ones. We experience dormant times and bursts of joy or blooming. Yet, sometimes we daringly wonder whether we are just pacifying ourselves, persuading ourselves that there is more to life or that life has a continuity that is not visible. I had doubted that the caterpillar would really become a cocoon, then had given almost no thought to the cocoon actually becoming a butterfly.

Maybe one of God's important powers is the power to transform living things. Most creatures undergo spectacular transformations. We humans are not only transformed in our bodies, in each new life stage, but also in our minds and emotions and spirit. These transformations take place in many people so many times and sometimes so dramatically that we are truly more authentically named as *changing* than as *staying the same.* We could claim that God as Persistent Life not only fosters transformation, but also enables us to "hold on" or "carry on" when we have given up on life, or forgotten the possibility that newness can emerge out of what seems like only death.

Quite a few times in seminary classes or churches, I have explained one idea of God's power as envisioned by the philosopher, mathematician, and theologian Alfred North Whitehead. He presented the idea that God encourages "the best that can happen" to come into being every moment, even after a tragedy. This theologian did not think that God is in control of every event, but did think that, in every event, God is persuasively trying to urge the best possibility to be born.

After the tragedy with our son, the one scripture passage that came to me as a kind of comfort was the one from the Gospel of John in which Jesus encourages his mother to consider his friend John as her son, and for his friend John to consider Mary as his own mother (John 19:26–27). I thought of this passage as prescribing a way to carry on. Yes, Jesus would die, but his family would carry on in a modified, adapted manner.

Two young women, lifelong friends of our children, spoke at our son's first memorial service in Irvine, California. They flew across the country to be with us and informed our daughter, Alexandra, that they were now her sisters. I concluded that they were my daughters. Since I had known them and shared so much time with them over the course of their lives, I was glad to be considered their mother and they my extra daughters. When I informed them that this new relationship meant they would now be the recipients of chocolate chip cookies from time to time, they said they could stand that consequence.

I thought of Jesus telling Mary and John that they were now family, of Jesus essentially giving them to each other. They might have found each other anyway, but maybe Jesus was not so sure they would take that step. I took this message to heart: "Carolyn, you can carry on, with family and adopted family members."

This message is only comforting if there is something meaningful to carry on. A new young woman friend, who lived on the same floor as our son in the college dorm, told a story at the second memorial service which was held in Dayton, Ohio. When she and Stephen went to a climbing wall to get some exercise, she asked him if he could climb to the top. His answer was, "Probably." They started up together, and in two seconds he had reached the top, while she was only two feet up. He came back down to guide her and encourage her. This young woman said that when she returned to the university, she would seriously try to climb to the top of that wall on her own.

I think this young woman was saying much more than her words may have conveyed. She was saying she would carry on, and carry on with some of Stephen's values incorporated into her life. Later, other people told me they had admired Stephen's conscientious-objection stance. They realized that they had not acted, as he had, on their views.

Whether it was our son's incredible warmth, his in-your-face frankness, his devotion, or his tendency to relate to strangers and break down barriers, the values Stephen brought to our lives are worthy of carrying on. In the face of grief, we don't carry on because life is lousy and we must put one foot in front of another, barely moving. We carry on because there is meaning and value in living, and people have shown us this. For me, I realized that I carry on with family and adopted family because I still have hope for a meaningful future, because life is persistent.

As much as I have gulped in grief and truly wondered whether tear ducts could run dry, the God of Persistent Life keeps transforming me, helping me to carry on, in part because my relationship with Stephen prods me to be part of the continuity of his being. We all have to envision a very different future than we would have enjoyed with him, a transformed future. Those who had a relationship with him continue, as I do, to have that relationship "inside." Meanwhile, since life is so persistent, though filled with startling transformations, Stephen himself probably continues his being in some transformed manner—beyond our understanding, but congruent with the persistence we observe about life.

Like the amazing butterfly emerging from the forgotten cocoon, nothing is lost in God, but instead undergoes surprising re-creations. Just when we think that nothing is happening, or when something or someone has died, we realize in an amazing way that the God of Persistent Life fosters some continuity with a twist. Innovation is constantly being born in every stage of our lives.

The Power of Shared Power: God the Jazz Band Leader

While I have used many of the metaphors presented in this book, and all of them have a place in the lives of particular individuals, there is one metaphor that I find the most believable and healthy for this historical moment: God the Jazz Band Leader.

The image of God as Jazz Band Leader connotes God's power and responsibility as persuasive and shared. It realistically evokes the experience of human freedom, with our power and responsibility, while also presenting God with enormous creative and persuasive power and responsibility. It is a metaphor for God that I find meaningful and practical.

In the cosmic "jazz band," God *does* lead; in fact, God is the most persuasive member of the band. Yet, God is playing, too, alongside us. God envisions how the piece will sound, how we will play our parts. God nods to us to take our turns, to slow down, to give others their turns. As Jazz Band Leader, God guides each band member individually, but simultaneously guides the group as a whole. God is not indifferent to what music is played; God wants to evoke certain themes (beauty, peace, love) through the music. But God enjoys the improvisations upon those themes that come from our creativity. Unlike the Orchestra Conductor, the Jazz Band Leader has no complete score toward which band members are lured or must perform. There might be an arrangement, but there is also genuine freedom for the band members—not just freedoms granted by the conductor, but freedoms built into the jazz music itself. Sometimes we humans listen a little, but ignore much, playing our own riffs as we get carried away with our own powers and abilities. Thinking of God as Jazz Band Leader is a way to envision our responsibility to play our part, acknowledging that we cannot expect God to save us in spite of ourselves.

I do not expect to see Jazz Band Leader used frequently in the litanies of church bulletins or heard often on the lips of those who pray grace aloud before meals. It is a shocking image. But that is exactly what makes it a good metaphor for God: it stops us in our habitual tracks and beckons us to rethink what God can do.

TRANSFORMING POWER

Whether we consider God as Lord of All or Shepherd, as Mother Hen or Potter or Jazz Band Leader, different kinds of power are tucked inside the metaphors we use. The implications are of no little concern. Our names for God affect not only how we relate to God, but also how we relate to each other: we tend to emulate the kind of power we assume God to have. We have too long held to God's omnipotence and modeled our behavior after that image. Now we need to consider God's power as shared power and persuasive love, and to model those qualities in our own behaviors.

If we go back to the question, "Can there be an all-powerful, all-good God *and* the existence of evil?" the answer is yes—if by power we mean "persuasive love," not "force to make happen."

I believe God can love, persuade, and cajole makers of bombs to transform their purposes. God can guide rational, thoughtful political leaders to see the effects of their decisions not just on their constituents, but on the world population. God can even transform—through guilt, worry, compassion, and self-transcendence—would-be terrorists. Yet, if God has the power of love instead of force, God cannot *make* the workers at the bomb manufacturer challenge their purposes, government leaders think compassionately for all, or would-be terrorists stop their behaviors. In other words, God is more like a Jazz Band Leader than a Puppeteer or Genie. God has the power to intervene *persuasively,* through love and wisdom, but does not have the power to intervene *coercively.* God's power is more like love and wisdom than a hammer on a nail. Yet, this is the very power that can transform and empower others.

One huge consequence of this view of God as persuasively powerful and wholly good is that it is understandable that we humans are genuinely free *not* to follow God's will. We are able to do evil or to act completely against God's will. God will mourn but not intervene to stop us. It is not that God is just "letting us" have this freedom, but that God cannot be other than how God is. God is persuasive and loving, providing wisdom patiently, persistently, and powerfully. God has no ultimate hammer up God's sleeve.

In this manner of thinking, God is completely caring, good, and the most powerful Being—using persuasive power. When evil occurs, we cannot blame God! We have to look at our own actions. We humans are the ones who have mucked things up, but we are persistently persuaded and loved by God to clean up the mess as much as we can.

We need to get on with our caring, with the power that we humans do have (knowing God is helping us along the way).

3

God Wants *What*?

God's Will

GOD THE DESIGNER OF ALL EVENTS: IS WHAT *IS*, MEANT TO BE?[1]

Undoubtedly, there are numerous times when one thing happens, then another, and then another, until we are amazed at how smoothly or surprisingly marvelous a relationship develops, a job unfolds, or an idea emerges. We think, *"It's meant to be!"* It seems so right to consider that God has helped to sculpt, weave, speak, or draw those events into being. It seems that God has willed the events, though of course we have cooperated, whether intentionally or not.

Among those who believe in God—and even those who are not sure of their belief in God—there is a strong sense that what exists, what *is,* should be. If it *is,* it is *meant to be:* If I am single at thirty, I am meant to be single. If I meet a person who wants to be my friend, at least for now, it is meant to be a friendship. If I find a job, I am meant for that position; if I do not locate a job, even that was *meant to be*.

Very often, when we believe that everything that *is,* is what *should* be, we believe in a God who both *designs* and *makes* things happen. The result can be that we drop ourselves out of the loop of responsibility and assume that God is able and does what God wants in all of our lives, all of the time. We think that humans simply adjust to what God makes happen. Or, without a belief in God, we think that "fate" makes things happen. Even from this vantage point, we are still out of the loop of responsibility. *Whatever happens is God's will.*

This is a very attractive belief. It can be quite useful, in fact, because it helps us make sense of the world. We may be either frustrated or happy with being single, unsure about what to do with this new person who wants to be our friend, or angry about getting turned down for a job, but these circumstances "make sense" if we can convince ourselves that they were "meant to be" that way.

Strangely enough, this belief subtly leads us to the idea that *all* is *good.* For, if something happens that is unwanted, we consider it as "good in disguise." How many times has a friend implied this belief when trying to offer us comfort when we are in crisis? After a car accident, it is not surprising for a friend to say, "I wonder what God was teaching in that, what lesson there was to learn," as if the car accident was *meant to be*.

Is everything that happens really God's will?

Think about death, for a moment. I believe that death is a natural part of life, part of our precious process of unfolding. When death is "natural," at old age, it can be beautiful, and often is. Death certainly can seem to be "God's will" when it happens in old age, or at the end of a very difficult illness. But I do not believe that all deaths, under all circumstances, are "God's will." When a person dies of a fluke accident, is a victim of violence, or dies from a curable illness, I think that God willed very hard for that person to live.

I am aware that to declare that a tragedy is God's will is comforting to some, for they can then view the crisis as having a larger meaning that we do not know. This understanding of God's will certainly may be right!

However, my sense of God's love and goodness and persuasive power leads me to conclude (along with plenty of other people) that things happen that are *not* God's will. This view can also bring comfort, with the knowledge that a loving God isn't somehow causing the tragedy. Our sense of a beautiful creation with creative processes that have some chaos, but much order, fits with tragedies as being just that—events that would have been best not to have happened.

From either perspective (considering everything that happens as God's will or considering God's will as thwarted and *not* happening sometimes), we can draw the same conclusion after the tragedy: God tries again very hard, and we can respond to make as much good as possible come forth.

If one person dies and another person blooms, developing heretofore latent talents seemingly as a consequence of that death, that is a blessing born. However, we do not have to conclude that one person's death *had* to occur or *did* occur in order to enable another person to bloom. The second person may have bloomed—or not—without the death having happened. Or, the second person may have developed in a different creative manner, if that death had not happened.

The position that there may be tragedies that are *not* God's will leaves us with the question, why *do* these unfortunate things happen? I believe that the simplest answer is that we have human freedom. God may be the Designer, but we have some say in how fully we follow the design, and we are influenced by factors other than God.

When there is a car accident, for example, and someone dies, we cannot say that the "fault" is entirely the driver's. Certainly the driver is responsible in many ways. But there are myriad other events that led up to the accident. We accept or reject certain speed limits and automobile safety standards at times. We choose to live busy lives and insist upon being on time. We multitask, even while driving. We accept less-than-the-strongest parts in manufactured cars. When we ask why there are accidents, we are helped by realizing that an amazing number of human decisions, which are not so apparent at first, go into each daily event. Human freedom that may waver from God's desired design can occur in tiny decisions that add up to a tragedy. God may be trying to get our attention even in all those little events.

We truly are free to follow God's guidance—or not. Of course, sometimes when we do not follow God's will, what happens is not necessarily bad or evil, it is just a different outcome. For example, God may have preferred that I be a math teacher, but I chose ministry. If God's wish, way back then, was not followed, I think that God has "gotten over it" and helped me every step in ministry. (However, since the idea of teaching math has not disappeared even after all these years, I now muse whether God has not let go at all!)

The truth is, it is not simple to know God's will. How do we *know* what God wants? It's not as if we get a ticker tape from God each morning with God's will for that day printed on it, God's preferred design. I do believe, however, that we can seek to discern God's guidance consciously by attending to the question, "God, what is your guidance?" I also believe that a vast amount of guidance comes unconsciously, whether we ask God or not (even whether we believe in God or not). I think God guides even those who *don't* believe God guides!

No matter what we believe about God's will, we can be comforted in knowing that God is right with us as and after tragedy happens and is designing relevant new ways to evoke good. God is trying to bring hope, redemption, healing, and new life.

GOD THE PROPOSER: DARE WE SAY NO TO A PROPOSAL?

When I turned fifty, I had a big party. (My twin sister was present, so we called it a hundred-year birthday party.) I asked women friends to come to my home to share with each other. We celebrated some of the things in our lives that had "borne fruit," things we had said yes to that had come to fruition. Women shared about children, gardens, meals, friendships, and jobs. Then we shared about some times we had said no. This sharing was far more solemn. The fruit-bearing discussion had been lighthearted and celebratory. The no-saying was more pensive. But these women were not necessarily sad about their noes. The no-sayings had been important aspects of their lives, just as the yes-sayings had been. Of course the noes had been less known among us, for they named events that did not happen, as a result of saying no.

During the course of a lifetime, we have thousands of choices to make among viable options. We may hold hundreds of different ideas about how God does or does not propose guidance for us as we choose. But, by midlife (some, of course, much earlier; some, at ninety), most of us begin to realize that we cannot say yes to everything and that saying no is sometimes wise, even perhaps divinely inspired.

When I was thirty and single, I knew I had chosen that state; I had said no along the way. Sometimes we say no to a potential friendship because we decide it doesn't work for us at the time. Sometimes we say no to a job that is offered to us because we decide we do not want it.

Is there room in our philosophies for a no to be the best answer? Or, do we hold a slight inner pressure to say yes to whatever knocks on life's doors, assuming that if it knocks, we should say yes because it was, after all, proposed? There are exceptions, but I think that many of us have a knee-jerk tendency to believe we should answer yes to requests, ideas, suggestions, and obligations. We act as if a yes is better than a no.

Our traditions celebrate people in the Bible who said yes. Esther is one of my favorite yes heroines. For heaven's sake, she said yes to saving her Jewish people. What a yes! She agreed to be scrutinized with the most beautiful women of the kingdom and then to accept the invitation to become queen, keeping her Jewish identity a secret, especially from the king. She did this in order to accept the huge responsibility to persuade her new husband, the king, not to kill the Jewish people. She succeeded, using both her intelligence and her courage. For centuries, the Jewish tradition of Purim has been celebrated annually, largely in honor of Queen Esther.

I think we sometimes overlook that there was an opening for Esther to become queen precisely because another woman had said no. It wasn't just any "no," it was a "no" to the king, her husband. There had been a very big party lasting several days, and on the seventh day, the king had asked Vashti, who was then the queen, to parade around yet again so the princes could see her beauty. To this final request, she said no. For that "no," Vashti was deposed as queen (Esther 1:5, 10–12).

It is understandable to think that Queen Esther should have said yes to the offer of becoming queen. After all, her position helped spare the Jewish people of that era. Is it also true that Vashti should have said no? In retrospect, we easily say so, for it paved the way for Queen Esther to say yes. However, at the moment when Vashti said no *to the king*, do you think that *she* was sure that saying no to a proposal, even a request, was unequivocally right? Or do you think that she was courageously declaring her stance not to be treated as an object, not knowing what the consequences would be? Even if Vashti believed that her "no" was God's proposal, I think it is pretty clear in the biblical account that King Ahasuerus did not think so. After all, she had set a terrible example for the rest of the kingdom, establishing a precedent that a wife could say no to a husband's request!

In our current culture, one of the most debated yes-or-no questions surrounds a fertilized ovum. Is there room for a "no" to be the best answer in this situation? Are we certain that every fertilized ovum is proposed by God to become a fetus, and then a child? Or, could it be that God's proposal for a particular ovum would be, all things considered, that it not develop into a child? Can we assume either one of these alternatives without knowing much more about the whole context? What is its health? What is the health of the woman, the man? What other life proposals is God offering to the woman and man, and how are these important to the world? Are there other children? What are the ages of the woman and man? What emotional security and resources can they and their community offer a child? What are the circumstances of the families, extended families, community, and world?

In a psychology of women course I taught at United Theological Seminary in Dayton, Ohio, we were discussing a report that appeared in psychologist Carol Gilligan's book *In a Different Voice.* Gilligan describes a study of women's decisions regarding undesired pregnancies, focusing on the women's ethical reasoning. After class, a woman talked with me in the parking lot about an abortion she had at age thirty-nine, after having had other children. She was in a real dilemma: how to choose viable birth control in her marriage given her particular set of circumstances. As she spoke, I realized that during all three hours of class, we had used third-person pronouns; we had said "they" and "those women."

The next week I asked each person to mark an *X* on a piece of paper if either she or he, the spouse, the mother/father, or daughter/son had ever needed to deal with an unwanted pregnancy. One hundred percent of the papers bore an *X.* We then proceeded to discuss the topic using the pronouns *I* and *we*.

There is nothing abstract about making choices with regard to birthing, adopting, or aborting. These are major life choices. The more we realize our responsibility for any potential pregnancy from the very beginning, the better. In my view, pregnancy resulting from rape or incest is very likely not God's proposal. I do not believe we should assume that the failure of responsibly used birth control that results in a pregnancy proves that a child was proposed by God.

The bottom line is that we cannot know with certainty that anything is *definitely* a proposal from God. We can pray; we can try very hard to grasp guidance; we can use community discernment. In the end, we face the ambiguity that either a yes or a no may be the wise response—even the one most desired by God—given all the circumstances. This is a much more complex philosophy than assuming that *whatever is, is proposed by God* or *whatever is, is our fate*. But it is a philosophy that recognizes the complexity of life.

Life is beautifully and dangerously ambiguous. It is for people with a grown-up sense of responsibility, for people who can consider consequences, even consequences for the earth and its potential inhabitants. Fortunately, we humans can be wise and responsible (though, we can also be irresponsible and foolish). Also, fortunately, we are not alone. We have each other to help us discern what to do. And, many of us believe we have Divine Wisdom that helps us to decide how to respond to all sorts of proposals in the midst of confusing times.

GOD THE IMPROVISER: HOW DO WE CREATIVELY RESPOND TO GOD'S NOD?

One Sunday morning when I was on vacation, our associate pastor, Rev. Linda Robison, was in charge. It proved to be an unusual morning. About ten minutes before the service was to begin, there was a thunderstorm (in Southern California!) and the power went out—no microphones, no lights, and no air conditioning. The man who was responsible for the sound came up to Linda and asked, "What is our backup plan?"

The church administrator of that Orange County congregation, Gail Kendall, had been in her position for about twenty years when I arrived. I quickly learned that one of her favorite expressions was, "We can always go to plan B."

Backup plans and plan Bs are reassuring alternatives to the intended plan. When a computer crashes, for example, it is reassuring to know you have a backup! Or when you have planned an outdoor wedding and the day brings a downpour, it is good to have a plan B.

I can easily envision God as having preferred plans for creation and God's creatures. Given our creaturely ability to use our free will and the difficulty of knowing God's plan clearly, I can only imagine how many times we do not follow God's "plan A." When this happens, we might imagine that God reveals "plan B."

As an alternative, I like to think of God as *not* having one plan with a backup, but rather coming up with something on the spot. God might truly improvise, providing a new plan based on the real possibilities that are feasible, given the current situation.

Improvisation is intentionally creating in the moment, without a fully premeditated plan. The improvisation is integral to the *creative process* itself. The creative process is intended; the outcome is not known in advance. To be clear, with improvisation, there is not a plan A, with a backup plan B.

That does not mean that improvisation is easy or that people—or God—are lazy or unprepared if they improvise. Actually, the reverse is true. Improvisation is possible if and only if you are very well prepared. Prepared, not planned. Jazz musicians need to know a lot about music if they are going to improvise successfully, for all the notes are not written down. When a jazz musician improvises, he or she does not just play the instrument without any form or structure. I have been told that the jazz player follows a planned chord progression along with the rest of the band.

This makes the jazz piece a totally different experience from a symphony performance. Can you imagine what would happen if the bassoonist in an orchestra stood up for her solo during a symphony and improvised? The conductor and colleagues would likely be aghast, wondering, "What is she doing?" In a jazz band, the leader, who is also probably playing an instrument, nods, and within the framework of the piece, the drummer or saxophonist takes off on a riff.

I read in our local newspaper that the New World Flamenco Festival was coming to town. Included in the program would be performances by a pair of famous dancers, Savion Glover, a Tony Award–winning classical tap dancer, and Yaelisa, a brilliant Flamenco artist. What caught my attention was that the artists indicated that their performances would be improvised, which meant that Tuesday's performance would be different from Wednesday's.[2]

The Flamenco dancer, Yaelisa, said, "People have said to me over the years: 'How can you go out there and improvise? That's so risky.' But I'm not scared. *How can I make a mistake if I don't know what I'm going to do?*"

I was enticed to learn more. Flamenco was originally something that people did in the streets, on street corners, just like hip-hop and jazz. As Savion Glover, the tap dancer, explained, "The streets are always changing. If it comes from the streets, change is the only thing that's consistent."

I know a terrific Orange County teacher of music and drama, H. H. Hanson, who has directed numerous musicals with teens. He drills performers with dramatic improvisation, and the students work hard to learn how *not* to know what they are doing—until they can *do* it.

There are some serious life lessons in this skill of improvisation. We may not always have or need a plan—let alone a plan B—but if we are going to improvise, we need both knowledge and trust.

I think of the time when Jesus told his disciples to go out as missionaries. He asked them to "be wise as serpents and innocent as doves" (Matt. 10:16). It seems he wanted them to have a good balance between wisdom and innocence, knowledge and trust.

Jesus continued with this comforting advice: "Do not worry about how you are to speak or what you are to say; for what you are to say will be given to you" (Matt. 10:19). That takes some trust! He went on to explain, "It is not you who speak, but the Spirit of [God] speaking through you" (Matt. 10:20).

What we ordinary people need to know, when we go about facing ordinary challenges, is exactly what Jesus told his disciples: we *can* know what to do when the time comes. We have many opportunities to improvise, to be creative problem solvers, and thinking of God as helping us to do so may not only make sense, but may also help us to lighten up, to enjoy life more!

The first time our son did his own laundry when he went to college, he stood at the dryer and wondered how to get all his clean clothes up several flights of stairs with the fewest wrinkles. His creative solution was to put on the clothes—all of them, in multi-layers. I do not think he planned that. He improvised. (If he had planned, he probably would have taken hangers with him.) At times, improvisation is not only necessary, it can add zest to life.

Plans and backup plans can be very reassuring. Planning ahead can be helpful; think lesson plans, building plans, meal plans, strategic-growth plans. However, improvisation introduces a certain *joie de vivre* to life—the joy of creating and engaging, the excitement of new possibilities.

I imagine that God is a pretty good planner. I do like to think God has plan A, plan B, even plan C. However, I imagine that God is at least as likely to be a terrific Master Improviser, able to take what is and help it become what it can be. When we say, "God willing," we might consider the scenario of God creatively improvising amid the current circumstances.

Many metaphors for God indicate that God is in complete control, even has everything all planned in advance, like the conductor of a symphony piece, but I do not experience life to be fully controlled by God. I do not believe that God can do everything by God's self. I think that view of the way creation works would be boring for both God and creation. Why would God want to place some massive DVD into the DVD player of the universe in order to watch God's own program play?

No. God labors, gives birth, nurses, comforts, and enjoys creation, with us. One of my favorite theologians, Marjorie Suchocki, writes in her book *In God's Presence,* "God works with the world as it is in order to bring it to where it can be."[3] I like that: God improvises with what we are, to help us move toward what we can be.

Because we may tend to restrict our thinking of improvisation to the realm of music, I present here a few vignettes that demonstrate one thing in common—creative improvisation in life. These scenarios may help us to see the *pervasive nature* of creativity, in the moment, which may, in turn, help us to think about God as Improviser, quite active in our lives.

Gardening: Keen Observation and Care

When I lived in the Midwest, I had good success growing tomatoes. I read somewhere that marigolds helped to keep bugs away from gardens, so I planted plenty of marigolds with my tomatoes. One year I discovered Dayton's original community garden, which had at that time enjoyed over twenty-five years of continuous service to the community. It is called Edgemont Solar Gardens now, and is near Broadway on the west side of town. The gardeners, led by the two ninety-year-old founders of the project, gave so much tender loving care to their plants that I wanted to purchase my plants there.

The volunteers I met suggested that I simply pick some marigolds and tomatoes myself, from the ground, where they had sprung up from last year's seeds. I could have all I wanted, free. That was a generous offer, but I was a bit reluctant, for when I looked at the plot of ground to which they pointed, I saw "weeds." Two older women decided I needed assistance. They showed me the jagged edges of the marigold and the slightly darker tomato leaves. Soon I was pulling out the two species confidently, glancing repeatedly at the samples these women had given to me to use as guides.

The women then began to plant the hundreds of seedlings I had chosen into a plastic tray they had pulled out of the "junk pile" of pots. I watched the efficient manner in which they placed all these seedlings into the tray at the same time, covered the shoots with dirt, then stood the plants upright in one motion. (I would have filled the tray with dirt, then planted each seedling, one by one!)

On the way back to the greenhouse, one woman saw a collard green coming up in the middle of the still-barren field, a "residual" from last year, she said. She pulled up that green to take home for dinner.

I marveled at the simple, profound, insightful, experienced, humble, yet authoritative manner of these two women. They showed me how we need to have both keen observation and care if we are to be attentive to opportunities for creative improvisation.

Families: Creative Integration of Cultures

Lois and Eunice are named as cherished women in the letter that Paul wrote to his friend and colleague Timothy in the Bible (2 Tim. 1). Timothy's dad was Greek, and his mother, Eunice, was a Jewish woman who had become a Christian. Her mother, Lois, had become Christian as well. Amidst this diversity of thought and culture, Lois and Eunice taught Timothy that God was within him, and that God gave him the spirit of power, love, and self-discipline. In a mixed family of Greek/Jewish/Christian heritage, Lois and Eunice improvised how they would live and teach their faith.

Quilt Making: Turning Scraps into Treasures

After clothes are sewn, there are always scraps. Those who sew a lot have bags full of scraps. My mother, Liz, and my husband's mother, Mary Nell, behaved as if they carried gold when they brought their scrap bags to each other! Consider the thousands of quilts that have been made from the leftovers of millions of skirts, dresses, and shirts. Quilts are beautiful creations, made from scraps, products of improvisation.

Cooking: Necessity Breeds Improvisation

Have you watched a cook in the kitchen who declared, "There is nothing to eat," begin to gather something from here, something from there, until dinner was ready? When we have a need and imagination, we can improvise.

Like gardeners, parents and grandparents, quilters, cooks, and jazz musicians, God excels at improvisation. I think God *wants* improvisation. I think God wants us to look for the marigolds and tomato plants amid the weeds, to find a way to live with a Greek husband and Jewish/Christian mother, to create dinner from "nothing." *God works with the world as it is in order to lead it toward what it can be.* That work requires improvisation on God's part—and on ours.

At college campuses it is said that half the incoming students list their major as undecided, and the other half just don't know it yet. We put a great prize on certainty, knowing, outcomes, but when we look back at our lives, when we note what is truly meaningful, significant, memorable, it is often those improvised days and evenings that come to mind with gratitude.

Just as we enjoy one another's creativity, God might be enjoying ours as well. Why not think of enjoying God's creativity, too? God gives us the power of love and self-discipline. It is a discipline of creative adventure, of beauty, of risk, of cooperation, and perhaps one of God's greatest features—improvisation.

GOD THE GRAFFITI ARTIST: HOW DO WE GET CLUES TO WHAT GOD WANTS?

If a friend at work said to you, "My days are numbered," or, "I can see the writing on the wall; my girlfriend is going to dump me," would you know that your friend was citing scripture? These expressions come from a discouraging vision that appeared on a wall in the ancient court of King Belshazzar (Dan. 5:10–12).[4]

In the midst of a great feast, Belshazzar ordered that the cups his father, King Nebuchadnezzar, had stolen from the Jewish temple be brought out so that he, his lords, wives, and concubines could drink from them. (Typically, when the Babylonians conquered a nation, they took statues of the people's God. But since the Jews had no statues of God, Nebuchadnezzar had nothing to steal. So, he had taken the vessels of gold and silver from the temple.) Drinking from those chalices symbolically emphasized the fact that the Jews—and their religion—were being held captive. Often biblical descriptions of leaders having huge feasts are intended to portray leaders who were living in excess, who were enjoying their power *over* others. Belshazzar was doing just that when he had a vision of a hand writing on the wall.

Belshazzar was terrified. His face turned pale, his knees shook, and he immediately called for the court enchanters, diviners, and wise men to figure out what the message meant. When the court magicians were at a loss, the Queen Mother told them to get Daniel (Dan. 5:10–12).

Daniel? Daniel *who*? It so happened that Daniel was a prisoner of war, a Jew, being held by the Babylonian leaders ever since they had conquered the Jews—and helped themselves to those temple vessels. The Queen Mother told of Daniel's ability to interpret dreams.

Picture this: Daniel, the Jew being held hostage, stood before Babylonian empirical power and made a side comment before offering an interpretation of the writing on the wall. Daniel spoke truth to power. He told Belshazzar that the Babylonian kings had usurped God's job. That is, the national leaders had killed whomever they chose. In fact, like some leaders of almost every age, they believed they had the power to choose whom to kill and whom to spare. Daniel argued that is the prerogative of God alone.

After this preface, Daniel read and interpreted the writing on the wall for Belshazzar using, essentially, three words: *tekel,* God "weighs" your choices and finds you to be a lightweight on the scales of justice; *mene,* consequently, your days are "numbered"; *peres,* your empire, which you obtained by conquering others, will be "divided" among others, who will, in turn, conquer you (Dan. 5:1–31). (It is interesting to note that all three words—*weigh, number,* and *divide*—are monetary terms used when exchanging coins. That's not accidental. Money language is the language that rulers of empires use, and God spoke Belshazzar's language—that of money and power—to get his attention.)

Basically, Daniel interpreted the writing to mean that there would be dire consequences for the way the Babylonians had been treating other nations and their peoples. There would be consequences for their imperialistic behavior—thinking they could rule the whole world instead of trying to get along with other countries. God's message was that their *behavior* was connected to the *consequences* of their behavior.

According to the biblical narrative, it ended up being quite a busy night. Just as the vision of what Belshazzar took for divine graffiti predicted, that very night the Persians conquered the Babylonians, Belshazzar was killed, and a new king was put in place.

When I imagine Belshazzar turning pale as he sees the handwriting on the wall, I visualize a student who is about to open up his or her report card, feeling a bit faint. He or she should have a good guess what the writing on the report card is going to be. It is not likely to be a surprise, for it is based on past performance. Belshazzar knew that he and previous Babylonian kings had been unjust and domineering to other peoples. Did he think God would be writing, "Congratulations!" on the wall? Not quite.

I visualize two extreme responses for a student with the report card.

One extreme response is the student who, when opening the report card, prays, "Make it all A's. I haven't done any homework, and I missed three tests, but please, God, make A's be on this piece of paper!"

The other extreme response is the student who has done a responsible job, working hard all semester, and opens the report card to see a C+. This student prays to God that she will not go to hell when she dies. She is very afraid, not only of her parents, but also of eternal consequences for her less-than-perfect performance.

Notice: both students pray! This is a theological issue. One prays for *reality to be altered*—for F's magically to turn into A's. The other prays to be *spared some imagined horrible fate,* even though her behavior wasn't terrible.

As I tried to consider what might be parallel for those of us who are fortunate enough to no longer receive report cards, it dawned on me that, in some way, doctor visits might qualify. We are told to do certain exercises, to eat or not eat certain things, to follow certain practices or refrain from certain behaviors. We nod, thank the doctor, go home—and either change our ways, or not. When we return to the doctor months later, we face with anticipation, sometimes dread, the results of new tests to find out whether our "numbers" are better.

I confess that I have been like the student who prayed at the last minute, "Make them all A's." I have prayed the night before a cholesterol test that my numbers had gone down, even though I kept eating butter and cheese. I have wanted the cause and effect of my behavior to be interrupted, for God's fingers to clean out my veins in some manner that would allow me to keep eating—at least cheese.

I am sure I am not alone.

We, like Belshazzar, sometimes want to be spared the consequences of our actions; we want the effect of our causes to be wiped away without us needing to wipe away our causes. Not only that, we often ask God to do this as a favor for us. We sometimes call it prayer. We do this on the national level, as well as on the individual level. Though we want God to be a Divine Rescuer, we may have been ignoring all the graffiti art God has been writing on our walls, trying to get our attention to change our behavior so that we do not *need* rescue.

Sometimes it works. At least, it *seems* to work.

Let us say we have a habit of running red lights. We persuade ourselves we are running yellow lights, but actually, they are red. We have run about a dozen in the past year, and we have been lucky. No accident. No ticket. Neither we nor anyone else has suffered a bad consequence for our bad behavior. We might manage to live with the same number of red lights run for many years and never suffer any consequence—except a slight dread and guilt just before and just after our infraction.

Cause and effect is complex and intricate. Many times we are spared the consequences of our stupid behavior, so we may begin to believe that God can and will interrupt the effects of our causes. The opposite can also be true. We can imagine consequences for our behavior that simply will not happen. Like the girl who is afraid of hell when she sees a C+, some of us are almost immobilized by guilt over any minor infraction. We are afraid of dire consequences. We accidentally run one red light, and we fear the consequence for six months, certain that any day a ticket will show up in the mail. Or we have one chocolate éclair and worry for two months about its effect upon our numbers. We are anxious about the effects to such a degree that we do not enjoy living. We have a hard time thinking of God as a Wise Counselor or Graffiti Artist, gently and creatively guiding us. Instead, we hold on to God in our minds primarily as a Judge, meting out punishments.

On one hand, lessons from history, biology, and our religion—including this narrative from the book of Daniel—demonstrate that we "reap what we sow," that "we are what we eat," that our behavior does lead to consequences.

On the other hand, we clearly know from history, biology, even our religion, that we—as individuals and as nations—are not expected to be perfect. Somehow, life has been created so that, even though one mistake can lead to horrible consequences, we often have plenty of chances to goof up and not suffer irredeemably.

To mix metaphors a bit, we can visualize God as a Divine Therapist, helping us look truthfully at ourselves, wanting to guide us, wanting us to grasp the messages that God the Graffiti Artist is writing on the walls of life, right in front of our eyes. As a good therapist will do, God the Divine Therapist wants to help us change our ways, to behave differently. In God's case, God probably wants to provide people who can help us, whether those are prophets, leaders of other countries, doctors, or our very own children. God offers grace and forgiveness, but God does not (I believe, *cannot*) keep all consequences from happening. Like a skilled therapist, God may work to help us see the possibilities, to make sure we know what our choices are, and even want us to make good choices, but we (as individuals and as nations) have to take responsibility for healthy living.

Had the Babylonian kings stopped their grabbing for power and money long enough to look at themselves, they might have been spared their outcome. There was a period of time when they could have changed their behaviors and altered their future. If these leaders had looked in the mirror, they may not have had to read the writing on their palace wall. They may have read the writing on the walls of their very own hearts. That is where I think God the Graffiti Artist writes, even today—in hearts and consciences.

We went to a baseball game in Philadelphia between the Phillies and the Padres. The last hit by a Philadelphia batter went so far into right field that it seemed sure the Philadelphia runner on base would get home and the San Diego Padres would lose. The Padre right fielder saw the ball go deep into the field and *did not chase the ball.* I was disturbed.

"Go chase the ball … the game's not over! Go after the ball!" I yelled.

My husband and our daughter sided with the fielder. In fact, they might have said, "The writing is on the wall." It was pointless. They persuaded me that the fielder was wise to recognize that fact and accept it gracefully. It would have been foolish for him to give a quick prayer asking God to make a strong wind alter the ball's direction.

That game was over, but the player could look forward to tomorrow's game.

4

God Interacts *How*?

Our Relationship with God

TWIN SPIRITUAL NEEDS

An African American university administrator noted with pride that his two-year-old son identified with black children in magazines and on television. His son seemed to be developing a good sense of self-esteem. The administrator also noted that the son's best friend was a three-year-old white boy. The father hoped that, as his son grew, he would continue to identify positively with African Americans and to have friendships with people of many hues.

It is the nature of being human to identify and affiliate; we are "like" others and "with" others. The degree to which we meet these needs for "likeness" and "withness" affects our self-image and our interpersonal relationships. But we are not just "like" and "with" other *people;* we also have deep twin spiritual needs to be "like" and "with" *God.* These twin spiritual needs are seldom lifted up as needs that we fulfill intentionally, but they are powerful needs, and we work hard at an unconscious level to meet them or may suffer when they remain unmet.

"Like" God: Identification

When we see people we admire, we tend to form an emotional tie with them and try to be like them. This identification process continues all our lives, and it starts early. When our daughter was four, she saw a ballet on television and rushed to put on her tights to dance around the living room while she watched the professionals perform. When her younger brother saw the applause she got, he joined in the dance, mimicking his sister.

Identification is an important part of personality development. Psychologists tell us that by the age of four or five, children begin to believe that they have some of the attributes of their parents.[1] For example, if a child believes that her mother is "important" and that other people "listen to her," the child is likely to believe in the value of her own words and thoughts. Or if a child experiences his father as warm and caring, the child is likely to relate to others with a parallel warmth and care.

Identification can empower us. We see another who is like us in some ways doing something quite well, receiving the plaudits of others, and we feel encouraged to reach for goals that we might have thought out of reach. African Americans gain confidence, greater self-esteem, and a greater sense of internal power when an African American runs for the presidency of the United States. Similarly, a woman running for president emboldens women to have a greater sense of their own value, responsibility, and power.

Clearly, identification is strongest when there is gender likeness or ethnic and cultural similarity. I experienced the strength of gender identification vividly when I heard a woman seminary professor speak at a gathering of clergywomen, at a time when clergywomen and women professors were still few in number. I had heard hundreds of lectures by men, but when I heard this professor speak, I experienced a new sense of empowerment. I had previously identified, to a degree, across gender lines with male professors, but identification with her clarified my goals and made them appear more attainable.

The process of developing identifications is not entirely left up to us as individuals. Our culture bombards us with images with which we are urged or expected to identify. Some of the messages are so insistent and so frequent that a degree of identification occurs without our realizing it. We think we have ignored or rejected images constructed by a particular commercial, only to find ourselves gravitating toward that product when we go to the store.

Similarly, when we are growing up, we may take pride in how different we are from our mother or father, how much of an independent existence we are creating for ourselves. Yet we discover that some of those attributes we rejected in our parents have become part of our own personality when we are older.

At times, the way a person identifies with others could be unhealthy. For example, I may want so much to be like my sister that I have difficulty deciding who she is and who I am. Also, it is possible to lose balance with our identifications. Sometimes, it is healthy to identify with the alienated, in order to stay aware of each person's need to belong. But it would not be healthy to always identify with those who are alienated. Likewise, we can benefit from some identifications with those who are admired, but if we *only* identified with heroes and heroines, we might be driven in a pathetic way toward perfection or success. An integrated balance of identification with various roles and role models helps us to lean into our own centered identity.

While many of us are preoccupied with identification during our teenage and young adult years, we can be affected by important identifications at any age. We continually encounter new images and new role models, and we discard or modify old, irrelevant identifications as we accept new ones. Identification is a lifelong, dynamic process.

Our relationship with God is also dynamic. However, because the Divine is so awesome to conceptualize, we grasp for identification by thinking of God as possessing some attributes that we can recognize. We might think of the Deity as loving, for example. The more we think of God as loving, the more we realize that we can be loving, too. We recognize that our love—between parent and child, between two lovers, between friends—is *different* from how we think God loves, but it is also *like* how we think God loves in other ways. We recognize that although there are many ways we are *not* like God, we assume that we are like God in some significant ways.

Obviously, identification with God in no way means that we try to become God or pretend that we are God. Rare people who over-identify with the Deity—thinking themselves to *be* God or having a difficult time distinguishing themselves from God—need psychological assistance! Though we need to recognize our distinction from the Deity, that we were made in the image and likeness of God is a major premise of Judeo-Christian tradition. We believe that we possess some godlike qualities that we are expected to develop.

Identification with God is in line with the teaching of Ephesians 5:1: "Therefore be imitators of God, as beloved children." Christian religious education teachers may start children on their journeys toward identification with an image of God by writing the word *God* on the board and asking for qualities that students think God has. Children may call out, "Loving, Forgiving, Wise, Fatherly, Powerful, Patient." The teacher is likely to proceed further in the lesson, suggesting that the children live out many of these godlike qualities, encouraging them to be like God in some ways, both emotionally and behaviorally—to love, to forgive, to live wisely. (Of course, there is no thought that the children should imitate God in all ways. They are not encouraged to think they could be everywhere present or that they should exert enormous persuasive power.)

I will come back to this in a moment, because our identification with God directly links with our metaphors for God, but first, I want to look at another side of the same coin: How do we experience being *with* God?

"With" God: Affiliation

Even in a culture that places a high premium on independence and self-fulfillment, it is obvious that we long to be with one another, to feel connected. "I want somebody to love," is the theme of pop music in every generation. Whether we are in pain or in a joyous mood, most often we want to be *with* others. Children run to be held when they skin their knees. Adults fly across the country to be with relatives who are having surgery. When we play a game, reach a goal, have a birthday, we want to celebrate with others.

It may be obvious, but it is worth noting that at each life stage, being with someone is a crucial need. The infant must be with a nurturer, must be touched, to survive physically as well as emotionally and spiritually. Many children at very early ages begin to beg their parents to let them invite their friends over. Teenagers spend hours on the phone talking with their best friends. We spend much of early adulthood focusing on friendships and potential mates. As we approach middle age, we often become more involved with younger generations, nurturing them and the world into which they will grow. As we grow older, we may finally have time to be with our loved ones more, but we also begin to lose some of those whom we have loved for a long time. Our need for connection with each other lasts a lifetime—and beyond. We feel the need to be with loved ones who have died, in our present experience as well as in our memories. Death itself does not separate us.

We have a similar need to be *with* God.[2] Most prayers, in groups or in private, begin with the reminder that we are with

God. We "invoke" the Spiritual Presence, acknowledging our desire for affiliation, whether we pray out of gratitude, in sorrow, to confess, to adore, or to ask. People pray, "Be with Susan as she goes through this time of trial"; "Be with Jonathan as he finds friends"; or "Be with the leaders of our countries as they negotiate peace." I have heard many grandparents pray for grandchildren with such words as "God, be with them as they go on their trip." Some people bid friends farewell by saying, "Go with God," *"Vaya con Dios."*

It is also accurate to say that most religions are communal, teaching that no one can be genuinely religious alone. Each of us shares, worships, works, and rejoices with others. Our faith traditions encourage us to celebrate the crucial moments of affiliation with those of our church, synagogue, or mosque. Children are baptized, blessed, or brought into the covenant of Abraham in recognition of their affiliation with the faith community. Weddings celebrate the bond of affiliation between two individuals. At funerals we mourn the fact that the beloved is no longer with us on earth.

Just as our *identification* with God (the living out of our "being made in the image and likeness" of God) is affected by how we imagine God, so, too, is our *affiliation* with God affected by how we imagine God. If we perceive God as a Judge, we may feel we are with One who judges us. If we see God as a Brother, we may feel we are with One who cares for (and teases?) us. If we understand God as a Whisperer of Wisdom, we may feel we are with One to whom we want to listen carefully, respectfully. If we think of God as a Choreographer of Chaos, we may feel we are with One who can help us with the really uncertain aspects of life.

Balancing "Likeness" and "Withness"

There are times when a person will be more aware of one spiritual need or the other: a woman making a major decision longs to be wise, like Divine Wisdom; a man experiencing grief longs to be with an Intimate Friend. When I was in the midst of a period of writing, I began many a prayer by calling God "Author," to help myself identify with God's creative power through the use of words. When I was lonely for a period of time, I stressed the fact that I was with God by beginning my prayers with "Infinite Friend." Both spiritual needs—to be "like" and "with" God—need to be met.

A clergywoman had served her local church for one year when she told a small gathering of clergywomen of her exhaustion. Some members of her congregation had become so dependent upon her care that she often felt like she was a "mama" to them. She said that she had felt a painful need for a mama to lean on. Then she remembered. She had one—a Divine Mama—she could name, pray to, and lean upon for support. *Likeness* to the divine image of Mama enhanced her awareness that she was *with* that very Presence.

The needs to be *with* and *like* the image of God are natural for all of us. Most of the time we do not think about these needs; we just use what images we are given and stumble upon meaningful ones along our life's journey. Sometimes, however, the light of life circumstances exposes the given images to be inadequate, so we search intentionally for new and broader metaphors.

Because a large percentage of the metaphors named and the images drawn for God in Western culture have been male and white, women and people of other hues have had fewer ways to experience themselves as being "like" God. Meanwhile, men may not develop their capacity to affiliate with God as fully as they might if they were encouraged to imagine God with many diverse images. Both men and women suffer from excessive use of masculine metaphors for God that suggest *dependency* upon an almighty being. All of us would benefit from fresh metaphors that imply *interdependency* between God and humans and get us out of habitual ways of conceiving God.

Diverse metaphors for God can expand our experience of God. For a black person, images of a black God might stir far deeper emotional and behavioral ties than images of God as white. Men who can visualize God with feminine metaphors might find they identify with God in new ways. A white person who imagines a multihued God can find new vistas, thinking of God in colorful ways.

Can you imagine what it would have been like for you if you had been shown a creative and diverse array of images for God, beginning when you were very young? How would that have helped you sense that you (and all others) are in some ways made in the image of God, *and* that you could come to trust that you (and all others) are also *with* God? Can you imagine what it might be like to use different metaphors at different times, such as Father in Heaven, Mother God, Creating Spirit, Spokesperson God, Infinite Companion, Lightning and Thunder Maker, Infinite Lover, and Divine Friend? If we, as a community, not just individually, used such diverse images, all people would have the opportunity to fulfill both of their twin spiritual needs.

I do not say this lightly, because I know old traditions and familiar terms feel comfortable. If you have been taught that God is _______ (you can fill in the blank, depending on your familial and religious traditions), it may seem somehow disloyal to imagine God in any other way than what you were taught. It may be precisely because our Intimate Friend is so intimate, that we are sometimes attached to how we name It. We often fear even *contemplating* change, but if we decide to explore images of God, there is much promise for a profound encounter with the Power that is beyond any one image or name.

God is beyond any one image or name! Yet, to live *with* (and to be *like* in some creatively good ways) that God, we image-making humans *do* imagine. It is in making those images foreground, not background, that we discover what we deeply believe about God. I believe that this very discovery is precisely what we need to make in order to live with each other—and God—responsibly in our world.

IMPLICATIONS FOR HUMAN RELATIONSHIPS

Only few in any faith, usually the most philosophical, manage to experience God in such an abstract way that they go beyond *any* image. For example, Vedanta Hinduism (which is the most philosophically abstract form of Hinduism) has few adherents compared to the large number of Hare Krishna followers and other Hindus who have myriad God images. Most of us, though we believe God is Spirit and worship God in spirit, have a metaphor tucked inside us that guides our assumptions about God's power, will, location, and knowing abilities. In order for us to consider God and God's relation to human beings, we use models of relationships that we know, that we have experienced. In other words, we ascribe to God human traits and actions that we recognize.

Greeks and Romans, as well as many others, gave gods personalities, projecting how they interacted with each other onto the skies. Our understandings of humanity affect what we believe about God. What we often do not think about is that this works in reverse: our descriptions of God affect what we believe about *ourselves*. Philosopher and theologian Mary Daly pointed out in *Beyond God the Father* that once we make God into the image of the Father, fathers are made into the image of God. Think about it; this occurs with every image of the Deity. Tell a nurse that God can be imaged as a Divine Nurse just as much as a Physician of the Soul, and (after she or he stops laughing), you may have improved that nurse's view of herself or himself over time. You may also have helped the nurse to find God.

The dominant model or metaphor that we use for God has many effects upon us. In subtle ways, we imitate the power and relationship that we have imagined God to hold. If we imagine

God to be distant, all-knowing, and almighty, our human interactions are thus influenced. If we imagine God to be responsive to us and affected by our responses, up close and attentive, our lives may more resemble harmony with each other.

A CLOSER LOOK AT ONE METAPHOR

How we respond to a God metaphor depends on what we project upon it, given our assumptions and our own experience. A metaphor may mean a different thing to each of us, depending on our associations. Take, for example, the metaphor of God the Coach. From many years of watching our children and their coaches (soccer, softball, baseball, and swimming), I have learned that calling God Coach can mean drastically different things for different people. For starters, each coach (as well as each parent and player) has a mental construct of "coach," a notion of what a coach is like, just as each of us carries a notion of "God" inside our psyches as we pray, enter worship, or talk about God.[3] Whether we have played on a team, been wildly cheering fans, or been somewhat passive observers—all these will affect our concept of God as Coach.

Throughout this book, I have explored metaphors for God, focusing upon the implications tucked within each for what kind of power God has and how these metaphors convey something about God's will—that is, what God wants. It is the same with God as Coach. Different coaching styles translate into significantly different behavior on the field, and different interactions with God when we pray or think about the Divine.

It *might* not matter so much what we believe about God if our beliefs satisfied only our inner spiritual needs and did not translate into our behavior and attitudes. But our views of God have effects *on other people,* effects that influence our interactions with others. Therefore, our belief in God's style of "coaching" matters, just as the style of our kids' coaches matters. How we assume the coach uses his or her power makes a difference. Our implicit assumptions about divine power, will, location, and knowledge, in turn, guide our notions of how all leaders, from parents to politicians, should act. This is why it is important to consider not only a variety of metaphors for God, but also all implications of those metaphors for our human relations. Within the metaphor of God as Coach, for example, are five (at least!) very different views of God that we could hold to, based on what our experience with coaches has been. Given my teenagers' avid athletic interests, our family has witnessed dozens of coaches, and I have used my real life experiences to create composite pictures of five possible coach metaphors. Though I limit this discussion to youth team sports, we could analyze many other domains for coaching styles—from singing, speaking, and birthing, to a new counseling approach that considers the professional helper a coach. We could also use the same kind of analysis for other metaphors—Father, Mother, Lord, or Shepherd. I am going to keep this discussion to sports coaches, but my hope is that this exercise will give you some ideas about how you can understand and explore your own metaphors for God in more depth.

God the Distant Decider Coach

Visualize this: Eighteen boys exit vehicles, large red bags over their shoulders. They gather by the sidelines of the soccer field, drop their gear, and begin to stretch out. Small gestures of greeting appear here and there. The coach takes note of any boy who is not there. Even if a boy is thirty seconds past the mandatory arrival time—forty-five minutes before the game—he will not start. The parents read, listen to car radios, then casually line up along the other side of the field. They know that they cannot speak to the coach under any circumstance. Their boys are "his" for the next two hours; he has told them so in no uncertain terms.

Two hours later, the boys and parents talk about the game in their vans on the way home: the high points to remember and the situations that brought frustration. Siblings make suggestions, players and parents complain about some of the coach's decisions, and they kick around a few ideas about how the team might work better as a whole. Yet, most acknowledge that the coach probably knows what he is doing; he has the bigger picture. They'll never know why he did what he did. It's probably for the best, they hope; they shouldn't complain, given their limited knowledge of the situations.

The coach doesn't regret not hearing the ideas generated in the transporting vehicles. He believes that he does know best. He considers neither the thoughts of the parents nor the ideas of the players relevant to his decision making.

This style of "distant decider" coaching has some discomforting similarities with prominent contemporary American notions of God. The coach in this vignette and the God represented in some of our common prayers and hymns share similar descriptors: in control and all-knowing:

- Almighty Loving God, why have you given me this load to carry? I am not coping. I know your will is that I obey. I confess I'm impatient. Please help me to accept your will so I can give thanks for this situation that is so painful today. Help me to see the good in this, to know what I am to do. Amen.
- Almighty and Powerful God, you are so wonderful, you have such majesty. You see the big picture, and I look out only from my own eyes. I dare not ask, for I trust you are already providing. Yet, I beg you to help us right now. Amen.

- A Mighty Fortress is our God, a bulwark never failing; / our helper he amid the flood of mortal ills prevailing. / For still our ancient foe doth seek to work us woe; / his craft and power are great, and armed with cruel hate, / on earth is not his equal ("A Mighty Fortress Is Our God," Martin Luther, ca. 1529).
- All to Jesus I surrender, / all to him I freely give; / I will ever love and trust him, / in his presence daily live. / I surrender all, I surrender all, / all to thee, my blessed Savior, / I surrender all ("I Surrender All," J. W. Van Deventer, 1896).
- Make me a captive, Lord, and then I shall be free. / Force me to render up my sword, and I shall conqueror be. / I sink in life's alarms when by myself I stand; / imprison me within thine arms, and strong shall be my hand ("Make Me a Captive, Lord," George Matheson, 1890).

I think these images of coaches and of God influence each other. Frankly, I think one of the worst doctrines of coaching is the pretense that the coach knows all. That formidably shuts off the one with power from having even the tiniest responsiveness to the athletes. Even a knowledgeable coach does not know everything; he or she cannot, for the players are people who, by their very nature, change. The boys in the vignette above may be experiencing situations (feeling extra energetic, having a toothache) that would be good for the coach to know. But a "don't talk to me" coach will never know. When the coach will not listen and will not inquire, but pretends to know all, vast possibilities for performance and relating are cut off.

A "know-it-all" God has its attractions. An omniscient God is what vast numbers of people long to have. It seems comforting not only to be known in the present, but also to imagine some Being that guarantees order and goodness by knowing what will happen in advance. Domination itself is sometimes taken to be a highly valued quality, to be imitated in relationships between humans and by humans in relationship to others, and even to the earth.

Eighteenth-century theologian Frederick Schleiermacher most straightforwardly represents this "all-knowing" position. For him, God is benevolent and almighty—that is, God has unilateral power. Whatever *is,* is God's will. We live in the world God wants, and God is good. Therefore, prayer that is dialogue or asks something of God is not advised; there would be no point. Scheiermacher acknowledged that believers needed that kind of prayer to make *themselves* feel better, so he tolerated it. However, the faithful, he thought, ought to simply give thanks, if they like what is, and pray to resign themselves to what is, if they are not satisfied. Schleiermacher cites Jesus in the Garden of Gethsemane, praying that the cup pass, until he resigns himself to the will of God (Matt. 26:39, Mark 14:36).[4]

The know-it-all model is occasionally satisfying to its adherents: the one who knows, or is assumed to know, decides for those who supposedly know less. There is no dialogue, but rather sheer obedience. (One famous coach who typified this approach was Vince Lombardi, who is said to have said that, for the sake of the whole team, he treated every player like crap.) The team may win games; the believers may feel comfortable. If what is occurring on the field and in the world seems decent, we can live relatively content with this theology and coaching model. While it is understandable that the "know-it-all" God would appeal more to those who are comfortable than to those who are in pain or oppressed, there is an appeal within this model to both. Those who are comfortable have a vested interest in keeping the status quo, while those who are in pain want to believe that a God who knows what to do can fix the pain or unjust situation.

The flaws in the know-it-all model become apparent if we begin to doubt the knowledge of the one in charge, or we begin to question the health of the power dynamic in the relationship. Then players/parents, or worshipers, are in a quandary. Do they challenge the coach/God? Do they try, through conversation or prayer, to communicate their viewpoints? If the coach/God has all-power (meaning the ability to make anything happen) and is at such a distance, how are players or parents in relation to the coach, and people in relation to God, to express themselves? Why inquire? It seems useless if we are not intended to have any effect.

Many people throughout Judeo-Christian history have acknowledged that it is okay to rage at God. The Psalms of lament testify to this strain of piety. Is the coach/God affected by that rage? Rage, if you will, in the van, but not to the coach's face—do not even try to have a calm discussion. Your kid may get kicked off the team, or worse—kept but held on the bench. Even if you do not care about the consequences, the ideas simply will not be heard.

This scenario points to another serious shortcoming of the Distant Decider model of God. An imagined all-knowing One is supposedly benevolent but is sometimes out of touch with those dominated. This God, like the distant coach, cannot know in advance what God's creatures are choosing. If God did know all our actions before we took them, we would not be free or creative; we would be puppets, clay pots (without "minds of our own"), or automatons.

Over the centuries, many in the Judeo-Christian tradition have believed in the model of a Distant Decider God. Many still do. Others think God is this way, but wish it were not so, longing instead for a more fulfilling God that fits the reality they experience. Some people are atheists because this is the God they do *not* believe in, and they do not have any other God to consider. They have not been introduced to a theological creativity that breaks loose from this almighty, all-knowing God at a distance. Still others have found other gods to make sense of the world we live in.

The consequences of our assumptions about the One "in control," lived out in our behavior, can be dire. If we picture God as Distant Decider, it suggests that our role is to do what God decides, and this emphasis on obedience can stifle not only creativity but also wisdom. The assumption of distance can also foster frustrations that we feel are not permitted to be aired straightforwardly—whether to God or to each other. If someone adopts this all-knowing position (perhaps even based on the premise that an all-knowing God "told me what to do, so I'm telling you"), it can be a rationalization for oppressive conditions. This model gone amuck presents some disastrous scenarios. When the one in charge sanctions the dropping of bombs from above, for example, as a wise expression of forceful power from on high, the rationale for following the one in control falls apart. Since the last century's world wars and holocausts, it has become more difficult to hold strictly to this idea that all-power and unilateral control equals wisdom and good.

God the Attentive Affirmer Coach

Visualize this: The girl wearing the number 3 softball jersey stands in the on-deck area, then moves up to bat. She lets a pitched ball pass. The coach asserts that the girl was smart; the ball was a little low. She hits the next pitched ball; it pops up and is caught; she returns to the dugout. The coach observes calmly, "Good try, fast run to first just in case; next time keep your swing a little more level." Another girl strides to the plate. She swings at a poor pitch. The coach comments, "Good energy; you're ready now. Be careful, though; that one was quite outside."

This "attentive affirmer" softball coach pays attention to every batter. On every single occasion, no matter what a girl does at the plate, the coach affirms some behavior. After the affirmation, the coach always mentions some slight improvement that could be made, relevant to what the girl has just done.

It is well known that affirmation reinforces behavior. Affirmation also generates a feeling of being appreciated, a mood of good will, and an openness to hear how to improve. Prepared affirmations have become available in multiple books and posters, recordings and websites. Affirmations are practiced by wisdom traditions throughout the world and are a core recommendation in such denominations as Religious Science, Unity, Divine Science, and Christian Science. But the appeal of affirmations reaches far beyond those formally affiliated with these denominations. It is comforting to think of God as an Attentive Affirmer, a coach who is knowledgeable, influential, and close by—not at a distance.

There are two implications of the Attentive Affirmer Coach metaphor for God to consider. First, we cannot be affirmed about specific behavior unless we have been *seen and valued.* Second, we need to be *receptive* to the coach's affirmations for them to be effective.

In order to affirm our actions and make relevant suggestions, the affirmer needs to be close enough to know us well. A coach who does not know us personally would be at a loss as to what to affirm or to challenge. There are multiple scripture passages that portray God as knowing us through and through, as being "up close and personal," caring about what happens to us, ready to "be there" for us. Here are just a few statements of affirmation in the Bible that reflect God's love and care for God's people:

- God, the Creator of the ends of the earth … gives power to the faint, and strengthens the powerless. Even youths will faint and be weary, and the young will fall exhausted; but those who wait for the Lord shall renew their strength, they shall mount up with wings like eagles, they shall run and not be weary, they shall walk and not faint (Isa. 40:28–31).
- Lord, you have searched me and known me. You know when I sit down and when I rise up; you discern my thoughts from far away. You search out my path and my lying down, and are acquainted with all my ways (Ps. 139:1–3).
- But now thus says the Lord, he who created you … Do not fear, for I have redeemed you; I have called you by name, you are mine. When you pass through the waters, I will be with you; and through the rivers, they shall not overwhelm you; when you walk through fire you shall not be burned, and the flame shall not consume you.… Because you are precious in my sight, and honored, and I love you.… Do not fear, for I am with you (Isa. 43:1–5).

In order to take in an affirmation and put it to good use, we need to be open and receptive to the affirmer's wisdom. In these examples, God is the invisible teacher, making available to us renewed strength and persuading us not to fear, but God does not *impose* this wisdom upon us. Personal action and receptivity are needed. We have the choice to "let" ourselves accept the guidance that God is giving. It is assumed that wisdom can be conveyed from God to humans; in other words, there is no great divide, but a kind of ready access, freely given by God.

In this Attentive Affirmer view of God, awareness, support, and guidance are key. Power "over" is not prominent. This coach/God does have a lot of power, but it is not coercive. Rather, the power is similar to that provided by a well of water, always giving when sought after, or like electricity, always available when turned on. This accessible power and presence generates an approachable, accepting, affirming mood.

Affirmation can be incredibly effective. When the United States Women's National Soccer Team won the Women's World Cup in 1999, Coach Tony DiCicco spoke about the enormous power of affirmation. He commented that he "recognized that the women responded superbly to challenges, but terribly to chastisement. Men can absorb tough criticism because they don't really believe it anyway. Women believe it and take it to heart. So I tried to coach positive."[5] He never showed replays of gaffes, but showcased the players' best moves and winning decisions. Each player was given a short video of her skills choreographed to music of her choice, and during the final week of the games, inspirational quotes were slipped under the players' doors every day. "This is not a female thing," says Colleen Hacker, a psychologist who worked with the team, "this is an elite athlete thing."[6]

The thoughts of theologian Paul Tillich have some affinities to this model. For him, God is the Spiritual Presence that pervades life. Humans receive from God and are shaped by God, with God functioning as Directing Creativity. There is mutual indwelling of one in the other. Though an affirming coach and a player do not "mutually indwell" each other, as Tillich views God and humans interacting, the Coach's advice and our receptiveness interplay with each other with a kind of creativity that is directed by the initiator, the Attentive Affirmer Coach.

God the Good-Guy Coach

Visualize this: The kids come from a variety of directions. A few are dropped off; some walk across the street from school; two take the metro. The coach smiles, greets the kids by name, hands out equipment, and they begin practice.

"Our goal is to have fun," he tells them. Five games into the season, with a 0-5 record, the coach encourages the kids: "Are you having fun? Sure you are. That was a strong kick. What a run you made; you're getting to be quite a defender. Chins up. We don't have to win; having fun and hanging in there together is our game."

The coach means very well. He has volunteered though he knows very little about the game, but after all, these kids need the same opportunities provided to the kids in the suburbs. The coach doesn't bluff or pretend to know more than he really does, but reorients the intention of playing to enjoying, not winning. For the most part, the kids do enjoy their time together, in practice and in games. Now and then they wonder, "Shouldn't we be getting better? Why are all the other teams so good?" Some of the parents and guardians think, "What a nice guy that coach is, but maybe our kids should have someone who really knows the game, who can help them actually learn something." Some grandparents reprimand those doubters, "This guy pulled together the team from nothing. He's always there for them."

Many people assume that, like this "good-guy" coach, God means well and truly cares. But they also go along in life without thinking about God very often. Life is relatively good; there are some frustrations, but that is to be expected. God is almost a volunteer who should be thanked for trying, for being there—but is somewhat innocuous. This might describe the God of "civil religion" in the United States of America:

- Mr. X ends his political speech with "God bless America." Ms. Y closes her address with "God bless you."
- "Ladies and Gentlemen, would you please rise for the invocation, and then this year's football season will begin!"

This Good-Guy Coach God is a feel-good leader. We the team have a coach who is, in a sense, "good enough." This likeable God is to be invoked—the more the better—but we do not think of challenging this God any more than the parents or grandparents in the vignette above would think of challenging their kids' volunteer coach. Besides, if we challenged or ignored this God, we might be thought unpatriotic.

Every once in a while, we may have dim thoughts that this Good-Guy Coach is not quite satisfying, not quite sufficient to meet depth needs for the long haul, but anyone who challenges the belief system is seen as too philosophical or not a strong enough believer.

Then tragedy happens—it seems the record is 0-5 with life crises. Followers of this God ask themselves, "Is this God sufficient? Does God make any difference in the world? Do my beliefs really apply to my life?"

In the vignette above, the volunteer coach has a good heart but not enough knowledge. However, I do not think that is exactly how we think about God, with this view. In the theological position that I am linking with this coaching model, God may *know,* but that knowledge is not practical because God *will not use* God's power.

In Rabbi Harold Kushner's book *When Bad Things Happen to Good People,* he takes a theological position that can be compared to this Good-Guy model of God. Kushner challenges our notion of a Distant Decider God, a God who is almighty and makes things happen. Having a child with a disease that led to premature aging and death, Kushner wrestled with how a good God could allow such a thing—a question that tapped into the feelings of millions of people who did not find bad life situations congruent with a good and powerful God. His conclusion is that God *is* good and inherently all-powerful (to make things happen), but that God lets humans have freedom to choose. In other words, God *limits God's own power,* and gives power to humans.

The conclusion, when a bad event happens, is that God is not to be blamed because, though God *could act,* God will not use God's power to intervene. Though God will not alter that limitation, God will always *be present,* no matter what. We can blame fate and various situations, but not God, for God wants only good. And while we mend from the event, God can indeed help us. God is there, comforting us.[7]

As I have mentioned earlier, I am troubled by this theological position because, for me, *being there* is not enough from a Being who *could* do more. I can laud a good-guy coach for being there for kids, if no one else is. However, if that coach is able to bring in another coach who knows the game and would be more effective, I would be pretty angry if he did not do that. I would wonder whether having that good-guy coach was getting in the way of having a coach who could really *coach.* In my opinion, the grandparents and kids in the vignette above are satisfied with too little. If it is possible, those kids deserve a real coach!

I would not be upset at God if all God could do is comfort. I would accept God as Comforter and would openly receive whatever comfort I could get, even when bad things happen. However, if God *can* intervene to prevent tragedies and does not, as a supposed "gift" to humans—that is, in order not to interfere with human freedom—then I am troubled. I would prefer a Comforter over a God who withholds "for my own good."

Just as I wonder about the kids' good-guy coach, I wonder whether an innocuous God of "civil religion" who is invoked here and there, but basically ignored as domestic policies and international relations are implemented, gets in the way of a serious God who is trying very hard, persuasively, to make a real difference!

God the Receptive Resourcers as Co-coaches

Visualize this: If you look, you can see them between every inning, helping the players hold the bat just a fraction more effectively, checking the equipment for a catcher, explaining a technical rule to the shortstop. You have to pay attention. These coaches aren't loud; they aren't obvious; they don't consistently yell out at the players—even with affirmations. Yet they are exceptionally wise.

These coaches work together as co-coaches, for they enjoy their interactions with each other, and they believe that their coaching is better as they dialogue with each other. Not only do they expect each other to have good ideas, these co-coaches include the players by asking them what they think is effective, what they think can be done to improve. These coaches even hold parents' meetings, asking for feedback and ideas.

Some might consider that these coaches have little power; after all, it seems at first glance that the players are in charge. The girls on the team even take turns coaching first base. But these coaches know that they have great power as they use both their ability to give advice to their athletes and to receive information from them, to hear the girls as well as speak to them. These coaches have huge power because they are effective in fine-tuning the players skills so that the players themselves are empowered.

One of the most striking features of this "receptive resourcer" coaching model is that there are two coaches in charge, as co-equals. There is relationality, even in the leadership. While this may surprise us as a model for God, the Bible itself includes a plural image of God. Elohim is one of the ways God is named in

Hebrew. It is plural, grammatically, but since it refers to the God of Israel, who is a singular deity, singular verbs and adjectives are used to accompany that name in scripture. In the Christian tradition, the Trinity is sometimes considered a relational dimension within God's self, but God, Three-In-One, is referred to as singular.

The mental image of co-coaches both giving and receiving (to and from the athletes) is also compatible with the view of God as present with attentive ideas and recommendations every moment, relevant to that moment. This God or coach may not be noticed—and certainly does not care for attention. This God/coach is anything but "jealous." This God/coach longs for us to grasp the good and wisdom that is available to us. This God feels empathically. Unlike God the Good-Guy Coach, the Receptive Resourcers Co-coaches God is powerful; the power is relational. Relational power actually increases as all are empowered.

- I know I am one of your many hands and feet, God. I want to make a positive difference in this world. I want to leave it better off than I found it. Help me to respond to loved ones and strangers as if all of them were you! Help me to see the little details as well as the huge picture, hurt feelings as well as broken systems. I am open to my role in this, God. Starter or relief player for you, star or backup, may I enjoy life and love that others are enjoying life. May I really see no one as an enemy. May I find you in all and help others to see you, too. Amen.
- You expect a lot of me, God. I humbly, almost bashfully, accept your mantle. I gratefully accept your help. Help me to have the courage,

> strength, perseverance, and love to do what I sense you are calling me to do. I trust that I am not called to "sacrifice" enjoyment, that you call me to love doing what you want me to do! May I stay focused on loving this journey. I accept your love.

Process theologian Bernard Loomer, in his insightful article "Two Kinds of Power," contends "that our lives and thought have been dominated by one conception of power ... power as the ability to produce an effect."[8] This "traditional view is the conception of power as the strength to exert a shaping and determining influence on the other."[9] This nonmutual, unilateral type of power is what a Distant Decider or an Attentive Affirmer God has. Even though one is more distant and the other more intimate, they both have power "over," and neither is affected by those "under" their power. Those understandings of God/coach perceive power as the ability to influence, but not also to be influenced. From those points of view, the idea of being influenced connotes only loss or lack of power.

Loomer points out an alternative: relational power. This power is "the ability both to produce and to undergo an effect. It is the capacity both to influence others and to be influenced by others. Relational power involves both a giving and a receiving."[10] A God with this relational kind of power has the capacity both to receive from another and to be influenced by that other. This receptive God would actually have more power, argues Loomer.[11]

To get a better sense of this idea of relational power, consider a teenager who asks her father whether she can go out. The distant decider dad would answer yes or no. The attentive affirmer dad would affirm some quality in the teenager, perhaps her good driving abilities, then challenge her to be wise. The good-guy dad might wish her well and send her off with a blessing. The receptive resourcer dad might wonder aloud what she is doing, hear her plans, and ask if she would like the two of them to consult a map together. His answer is dependent upon her plans and her thoughts; he does not have a ready-made answer. He might even ask whether she really wants to go out. In other words, he is helping her to make a wise choice, freely giving of what he knows but not pretending to know what is best for her, especially before hearing her.

Basketball coach Phil Jackson is an example of a Receptive Resourcer. When he was coach of the Chicago Bulls, he seems to have worked in this manner with Michael Jordan, helping Jordan to coordinate his talents with his teammates. Jackson is said to have listened to and received insight from Jordan in the process. Clearly, this relational leadership did not diminish Jackson's "power." Rather, the whole team benefited.

I think this Receptive Resourcers Co-coaches metaphor for God is brilliant. Not only do I think it is essential for the believability of God, but it also is important for all power structures around the world. I believe that, in our interactions with each other, we are wise to grasp the significance of *not* having to know all, of *not* being the sole dispenser of influence, but rather internalizing the value of learning and receiving from those over whom we are expected to have power.

God the Team Transformer Coach

Visualize this: The star high school senior works desperately hard to set up plays so that the younger people on the team can gain experience making goals. He passes the ball to one and then another, hoping to assist them in making goals. He repeatedly sets up assists until, eventually, his teammates do make goals. They gain a sense of what it takes and begin to expect to make goals. The senior cares much more about the team, how it will function, than his own number of goals. (He has made plenty!) An interesting phenomenon occurs: not only do the younger players gain experience making goals, but they get into the practice of setting up assists for each other. They have seen the selflessness of the respected player who knows they can win only if they work as a team against tough opponents, so their mindset becomes truly team oriented.

In order for team members to move into this "team transformer" model, they need a large shift in thinking. Many sports teams never make this shift, but the very good ones usually have to. The one in charge—that is, the coach—not only attends, affirms, teaches, listens, influences, and is influenced, but also works consistently toward team building. Not only has the coach grasped that the *coach's* power is increased the more the players experience power, but the *players* have grasped that they, too, are empowered only as their fellow players are empowered, as they work as one body.

Imagine a Super Bowl game in which a coach manages to transform the consciousness of the team so that each member fully grasps that he can play extraordinarily well against the team's skillful opponents only if the team works together at a very deep level. Each team member has to yield his own self-preoccupation in order to gain a team consciousness.

The quarterback expands his horizons, realizing he can make successful passes to several players, not just the one superstar. The receivers are not possessive; it matters most to them that *someone* catches the football. They work as one body, transformed from individuals performing at their peak to a team with a unified purpose. Strangely enough, when the coach manages to get this to happen, we who observe the game may not think about the coach. The coach is not dominant now—for, indeed, the coach has managed to empower each player not only with personal confidence but with a joy in thinking from the perspective of the whole. During the game, the coach calls the plays, but the coach is *not* in control, and the coach knows this. Those on the football field have genuine freedom, but they are attuned to the wisdom of the coach and the coach's trust in them.

This is a much more complex position than simply intending the good of all. It requires consistent effort to experience the "community self" as well as the "individual self," something very difficult for us Americans. (African seminary students consistently told me that in many parts of Africa, the collective self is the dominant identity.) It is not enough to have affirmed, empowered *individuals*. To truly win and enjoy the game, players need to care about each other, to work with sublime cooperation, with minimal competition amongst themselves, and to strategize *together*. This model brings forth enormous creativity.

When we make a similar shift in our thinking and begin to conceptualize God as Team Transformer, we see God not as in control, but as seeking in every fraction of a second to get us to pass back and forth to each other—even across amazing boundaries—until we all benefit. In this framework, God gives guidance to each individual, and that guidance dovetails for the good of all.

- Very truly, I tell you, the one who believes in me will also do the works that I do and, in fact, will do greater works than these (John 14:12a).
- My turn, God? Help me know what to do here! Thank you immeasurably for giving me this precious child. Thank you for guiding me for umpteen years so far. Help me now not to be afraid. Help me to walk between worry and trust, so I guide and am silent in right measure at the best times. I know you give Wisdom yourself to him (her). Please help him (her) to notice that Wisdom, to pay attention. May I grow through these years, even as

he (she) does. May I know how to guide at the same time I accept your guidance.

- God, I know I do not have to do it all. So many others are here to help! Please show me how to let go, to turn to others, to believe in others. Please persuade me to ask and to act at the right times. Why do I feel so responsible? We're all in this—along with you! Help me to trust you.

I am reminded of the terms *centripetal force* and *centrifugal force* that pastoral theologian Gordon Jackson uses to imagine God's will, both for individuals within a family and the family as a whole. Individuals may pray for "God's will" for themselves, seeking earnestly to know what path to follow. However, there may be conflict when what the individual believes she is called to do does not seem to fit with the needs of the family. Jackson suggests that God wills for *individuals* with a kind of centrifugal force, pulling them outward, and wills for *communities* with a centripetal force, holding them together. To fine-tune discernment at both levels may not be easy, but it is helpful to imagine guidance occurring for both at the same time, in a manner that maximizes satisfaction for all.[12]

Earlier in this chapter, I spoke about Coach Tony DiCicco and psychologist Colleen Hacker using the Attentive Affirmer Coach approach with the USA Women's Soccer Team. In addition, they trained the athletes using some strong team-transforming methods. The women engaged in trust exercises that required them to move blindfolded, and they practiced exercises that required them to move in symmetry as a team with balloons held between their bodies.[13]

Did you know that when each of the four members of a barbershop quartet hits a note perfectly, they call it "busting a chord"? I think this is a little like the harmony a team hits when they play together magnificently. Of course, this experience of harmony *could* occur for a team that has a coach who uses any of the five coaching styles I have presented: The Distant Decider Coach may make wise decisions. Players may follow and trust in him sufficiently that the members do truly work together; they unify at times. The team of the Attentive Affirmer Coach may experience moments of functioning exceptionally well together. The players each feel good enough about themselves that they find a larger whole. Players of the Good-Guy Coach may get into a "zone" of enjoyment so that they synchronize their actions. The team led by the Receptive Resourcers Co-coaches may rise to the occasion, talking with each other, listening to each other and the coaches.

But when it comes to metaphors for God, the Team Transformer Coach is a beautiful model of power, location, and knowledge that leads not just to moments of "busting a chord," but to, more often than not, permeating the game of life. The Team Transformer God engenders consistent self-transcendence—movement out of ourselves. While this is not a simple task, there are many ways a Team-Transforming Coach can generate a supra-conscious awareness of the other team members: frequent commenting on the position of other players, providing group challenges as well as individual ones, praising and giving incentives for attention to others.[14] Likewise, a Team-Transforming God would joyously expand our views on a consistent basis, moving away from individualistic views of spirituality to goals that connect us strongly with others.

CONCLUSION: METAPHORS MATTER

An op-ed piece in the *Los Angeles Times* caught my attention. It was entitled "Multiple-Choice God: New Survey Reveals That Americans Believe in Four Basic Types of Deity."[15]

The editor described a survey that had been conducted by the Gallup Organization for Baylor University. The results of the survey showed that 85 to 90 percent of Americans believed in God. However, what I found amazing was that the survey contained only *four* options for people to check as to what sort of God they believed in. These were labeled, not surprisingly, A, B, C, and D.

Choice A was for what they called the "Authoritarian God," who is highly involved with humans and "capable of meting out punishment."[16] A little over 31 percent of those surveyed believed in this Authoritarian God.

Choice B was what they called the "Benevolent God," and 25 percent of the survey takers checked that they believed in this God. This God "is involved in human affairs ... offers a positive influence in the world, and is less willing to condemn or punish individuals."[17]

Choice C they called the "Critical God," who "really does not interact with the world" and "will punish evildoers 'in another life.'"[18] The number of people who chose this option was almost equal to those who chose the Benevolent God: 23 percent.

The fourth option, D, was chosen by 16 percent of the respondents. It was the "Distant God" who "set the laws of nature in motion," but "has no interest in human activities."[19]

There were also people who identified themselves as "atheists"—5.2 percent of the survey takers.

When I read about this survey, I was distressed—as was the editor. I thought to myself, "There are other options for belief than these four!" That is what the editor thought, too, concluding, "If it does nothing else, the Baylor survey should lead to more sophisticated reporting."[20] Might not the options have included, even for those who do believe in God, "None of the Above"? Or, perhaps, "All of the Above"? Plenty of people who believe in God find their views of God not neatly fitting into any of those four descriptions. Thinking about and believing in God is very complex. I am saddened that people think that believing in God means believing in one—or even four—options.What is God like? The technical term for not being able to describe God is to say that God is "ineffable." My question is this: if God cannot be described, then why should we settle for *easy descriptions*?

Not long after this survey appeared, I heard a curious question raised on a National Public Radio program. The query over the airwaves was, "Describe the voice of Sean Connery, Odette, or Bob Dylan." One person said that Sean Connery's voice "sounds like a man who knows the outcome of the race before it's been run." Another person said Sean Connery's voice sounds like "the sensation of dipping your hand into a big black bag of marbles." I thought, "Say *what*? His voice sounds like knowing the outcome of a race? Putting your hand into a bag of marbles? What are these people *thinking*?" But I did agree, somewhat, with a third listener's response: Sean Connery's voice sounds like "wearing your boyfriend's dinner jacket on a cold night." Surely, some other listeners found that description absurd.

None of the people who described the sound of Sean Connery's voice was "wrong." All were using their own words to provide a description that pointed to a truth no one could fully describe.

If a familiar human voice that we humans can actually *hear* is difficult to describe or come to an agreement about, then it makes total sense that we humans have trouble describing God and that we come up with options at least as varied as those for Sean Connery's voice!

We have many choices of ways to think about God: Infinite Companion, Lightning and Thunder Maker, Prince of Peace, Creating Spirit, Womb of Life, Heavenly Father, Coauthor of Life Divine, Black God, Infinite and Intimate Friend, Divine Friend, Holy Breath, Shelter from the Storm, Light, Spirit of

Life, Compass, Wisdom, Bakerwoman God, Grandmother God, Lord, Lord of Lords, Author of Life, Comforter, Physician of the Soul, Mother-Father God, Choreographer of Chaos. *Monotheism is a belief in one God, not a belief in one metaphor.* We need multitudes of metaphors if we are going to aim toward the One.

As we explore our responses, we might want to ask, "What metaphors match my beliefs?"; "What metaphors would help me *relate* to this God I believe in?"; and "What metaphors might help me *expand* my belief?"

I want to go back for a moment to something I said at the beginning of the book: *We do not have to let go of one sense of God to include another. Neither do we need to go about challenging old metaphors. What is crucial is to find what metaphors grasp or aim closely toward what we really believe about God. When we find a metaphor—or two, or six—that creatively points toward what we believe, God can become so much more alive and meaningful for us.*

When I ask myself, "What metaphor can I use to convey what I believe about God and how God interacts with the world?" I appreciate thinking of God as Divine Jazz Band Leader. This metaphor fits my belief about God's power and responsibility in relation to ours. The Jazz Band Leader cares deeply, pays enormous attention to the band members, and plays alongside the members, but is truly guiding—never sitting out. The Jazz Band Leader, while having the most power and wisdom in the band, cannot make the drummer stop if the drummer keeps going. The Jazz Band Leader cannot coax a bashful saxophonist to play a riff if she does not believe she can. This metaphor implies genuine human freedom. I also appreciate the Team Transformer Coach metaphor, but it is less useful because it requires so much explanation! A third metaphor for God that works for me requires barely any explanation and is always wonderful: Love.

Theologians discuss the intricacies of God's power and God's will ad infinitum, but all this thinking is bundled tightly into a tiny package when we point to God with a metaphor.

Metaphors matter.

Metaphor wondering is a healthy way of thinking about God that evokes a joyous second-take: "God the *What*?"

EPILOGUE

Personal Metaphor Wondering

To help you find the metaphors for God that fit for you and echo your beliefs, I have compiled a God Belief Checklist and a God Metaphor Checklist. I encouraged you to fill out the God Belief Checklist *before* you read this book. Your responses will serve as a good reference, to see whether your thinking about God changes over time.

Now that you have finished your reading, fill out God Metaphor Checklist 1. This checklist includes metaphors presented in the book that will make more sense to you now that you have read *God the* What?

I recommend that you hold on to God Metaphor Checklist 2 until about a year from now, and then fill it out. Since both God Metaphor Checklists are identical, they can provide a useful tool to see whether any of your thoughts about God have shifted over a period of time or a change of circumstances.

Each checklist works the same way: read each statement and give it some thought, then check the response that best fits *your* perspective at the time:

- For the most part, I don't think this is true.
- This is not *my* experience, although I know others for whom this is true.
- Interesting idea; I might consider this.
- I sometimes think this is true.
- I often think this way.
- This is one of my core beliefs.

Your responses will likely be a mixture of what you have been taught, what your life experience has been, and where you are in your spiritual exploration at the moment—all the while knowing that, because you are human, your responses will change, depending on the day and the circumstances.

Your responses are not a theological declaration but a personal exploration. As I emphasize throughout this book, a God metaphor is *not* an effective metaphor if your response is *only* agreement with that metaphor or *only* disagreement. Metaphors function best when you have both responses: "Well, God might be like that ... but not exactly like that ..."

The goals of the checklists are (1) to help you consider how the metaphors you currently use for God align with your beliefs about God, and (2) to explore where your beliefs about God might open the door to some new metaphors.

Remember, we are talking about *ideas* about God. God is whatever God is. We are not changing that, but we have the right and responsibility to keep God-wrestling until we find ways of thinking about God—especially God's power and way of relating to us—that are intellectually and emotionally satisfying.

What do you think? Are you ready to do a little personal metaphor wondering?

GOD BELIEF CHECKLIST

Date ________________

I don't think this is true.	This is not *my* experience.	Interesting idea; I might consider it.	I sometimes think this is true.	I often think this way.	This is one of my core beliefs.	
☐	☐	☐	☐	☐	☐	1. God is in charge, all-knowing, and all-powerful to make things happen.
☐	☐	☐	☐	☐	☐	2. God is in charge, but chooses to restrain power at times, allowing humans to have freedom.
☐	☐	☐	☐	☐	☐	3. God keeps working on us, shaping us.
☐	☐	☐	☐	☐	☐	4. God and humans share power and responsibility.
☐	☐	☐	☐	☐	☐	5. God is steady, always there.
☐	☐	☐	☐	☐	☐	6. God understands and loves us, patiently, tenderly, forever, no matter what.
☐	☐	☐	☐	☐	☐	7. God comforts us, protects us.
☐	☐	☐	☐	☐	☐	8. God takes what is, again and again, and seeks to create the best out of it.
☐	☐	☐	☐	☐	☐	9. God encourages us to be the best we can be.
☐	☐	☐	☐	☐	☐	10. God knows our limits and works with us to use our potential as fully as we can.
☐	☐	☐	☐	☐	☐	11. God takes care of us.

I don't think this is true.	This is not *my* experience.	Interesting idea; I might consider it.	I sometimes think this is true.	I often think this way.	This is one of my core beliefs.	
☐	☐	☐	☐	☐	☐	12. God catches us or rescues us if we get into trouble.
☐	☐	☐	☐	☐	☐	13. God helps us to navigate through difficult waters.
☐	☐	☐	☐	☐	☐	14. God gives us strength.
☐	☐	☐	☐	☐	☐	15. God watches and assesses our every action.
☐	☐	☐	☐	☐	☐	16. God wants the best for us, but is not perfect.
☐	☐	☐	☐	☐	☐	17. God offers wisdom and ideas.
☐	☐	☐	☐	☐	☐	18. God influences us *and* is influenced by us; God motivates us to interact with each other, to support and empower each other.
☐	☐	☐	☐	☐	☐	19. God relates to each of us personally; there are no "one size fits all" responses from God.
☐	☐	☐	☐	☐	☐	20. God hovers over us, and is there to help.
☐	☐	☐	☐	☐	☐	21. God created the beautiful earth and everything good in it.
☐	☐	☐	☐	☐	☐	22. God is always with us.
☐	☐	☐	☐	☐	☐	23. God *is*.
☐	☐	☐	☐	☐	☐	24. God improvises.

Add your own thoughts and beliefs:

25. ______________________________

26. ______________________________

27. ______________________________

28. ______________________________

29. ______________________________

30. ______________________________

GOD METAPHOR CHECKLIST 1

I don't think this is true.	This is not *my* experience.	Interesting idea; I might consider it.	I sometimes think this is true.	I often think this way.	This is one of my core beliefs.	Date ____________
☐	☐	☐	☐	☐	☐	1. God is in charge, all-knowing, and all-powerful to make things happen. *(Lord, Almighty, "How Great Thou Art," Magic Wand, God as Genie, Distant Decider Coach ...)*
☐	☐	☐	☐	☐	☐	2. God is in charge, but chooses to restrain power at times, allowing humans to have freedom. *(Post-heroic CEO, Tough Love Parent ...)*
☐	☐	☐	☐	☐	☐	3. God keeps working on us, shaping us. *(Divine Potter, Divine Author, Bakerwoman God, Creating Spirit, Directing Creativity, Seamstress ...)*
☐	☐	☐	☐	☐	☐	4. God and humans share power and responsibility. *(Coauthor, Receptive Resourcers as Co-coaches, Jazz Band Leader, Dance Partner, Intimate and Infinite Friend ...)*
☐	☐	☐	☐	☐	☐	5. God is steady, always there. *(Rock, Best Friend, Divine Companion, Fountain of Living Water, Good-Guy Coach, Ground of Being, Presence, Mighty Fortress, Silent Partner, Holy Breath, Bright Night Light ...)*

I don't think this is true.	This is not *my* experience.	Interesting idea; I might consider it.	I sometimes think this is true.	I often think this way.	This is one of my core beliefs.	
☐	☐	☐	☐	☐	☐	6. God understands and loves us, patiently, tenderly, forever, no matter what. *(Dynamic Love, Mother-Father God, Sister God, Brother God, Grandmother God ...)*
☐	☐	☐	☐	☐	☐	7. God comforts us, protects us. *(Daddy, Abba Mia, Divine Mama, Comforter, Consoler, Shelter from the Storm, Womb of Life, Mother Hen ...)*
☐	☐	☐	☐	☐	☐	8. God takes what is, again and again, and seeks to create the best out of it. *(Choreographer of Chaos, Healer, Improviser, Divine Physical Therapist, Creative-Nurturing God ...)*
☐	☐	☐	☐	☐	☐	9. God encourages us to be the best we can be. *(Attentive Affirmer Coach, Creating Spirit ...)*
☐	☐	☐	☐	☐	☐	10. God knows our limits and works with us to use our potential as fully as we can. *(Divine Physical Therapist, Caregiver ...)*
☐	☐	☐	☐	☐	☐	11. God takes care of us. *(Physician of the Soul, Divine Nurse, Caregiver, Spokesperson God ...)*
☐	☐	☐	☐	☐	☐	12. God catches us or rescues us if we get into trouble. *(Mother Eagle, Rescuer ...)*
☐	☐	☐	☐	☐	☐	13. God helps us to navigate through difficult waters. *(Compass, Sail, and Wind ...)*

I don't think this is true.	This is not *my* experience.	Interesting idea; I might consider it.	I sometimes think this is true.	I often think this way.	This is one of my core beliefs.	
☐	☐	☐	☐	☐	☐	14. God gives us strength. *(Nursing Mother God, Persistent Life …)*
☐	☐	☐	☐	☐	☐	15. God watches and assesses our every action. *(Judge, King …)*
☐	☐	☐	☐	☐	☐	16. God wants the best for us, but is not perfect. *(Caregiver over Thirty-Five Accepting Her/His Own Ambiguity …)*
☐	☐	☐	☐	☐	☐	17. God offers wisdom and ideas *(Creative Wisdom, Graffiti Artist, Improviser, Divine Whisper …)*
☐	☐	☐	☐	☐	☐	18. God influences us *and* is influenced by us; God motivates us to interact with each other, to support and empower each other. *(Receptive Resourcers as Co-coaches, Team Transformer Coach, Jazz Band Leader …)*
☐	☐	☐	☐	☐	☐	19. God relates to each of us personally; there are no "one size fits all" responses from God. *(Divine Blacksmith …)*
☐	☐	☐	☐	☐	☐	20. God hovers over us and is there to help. *(Helicopter God, Grandmother God …)*
☐	☐	☐	☐	☐	☐	21. God created the beautiful earth and everything good in it. *(Creator, Author of Life, Poet of the Universe, Composer)*

I don't think this is true.	This is not *my* experience.	Interesting idea; I might consider it.	I sometimes think this is true.	I often think this way.	This is one of my core beliefs.	
☐	☐	☐	☐	☐	☐	22. God is always with us. *(Shekinah, Divine Presence, Infinite Friend, Light, Helicopter God, Uncountable Infinity ...)*
☐	☐	☐	☐	☐	☐	23. God *is.* *(The Power of Pure Being, Spirit, Breath, Music Itself, Ground of Being, Spiritual Presence, Directing Creativity, Beingness, "I AM," Uncountable Infinity ...)*
☐	☐	☐	☐	☐	☐	24. God improvises. *(Divine Jazz Band Leader, Divine Gardener ...)*

Add your own thoughts, beliefs, and metaphors:

25. ______________________________

26. ______________________________

27. ______________________________

28. ______________________________

29. ______________________________

30. ______________________________

GOD METAPHOR CHECKLIST 2

Date________________

I don't think this is true.	This is not *my* experience.	Interesting idea; I might consider it.	I sometimes think this is true.	I often think this way.	This is one of my core beliefs.	
☐	☐	☐	☐	☐	☐	1. God is in charge, all-knowing, and all-powerful to make things happen. *(Lord, Almighty, "How Great Thou Art," Magic Wand, God as Genie, Distant Decider Coach ...)*
☐	☐	☐	☐	☐	☐	2. God is in charge, but chooses to restrain power at times, allowing humans to have freedom. *(Post-heroic CEO, Tough Love Parent ...)*
☐	☐	☐	☐	☐	☐	3. God keeps working on us, shaping us. *(Divine Potter, Divine Author, Bakerwoman God, Creating Spirit, Directing Creativity, Seamstress ...)*
☐	☐	☐	☐	☐	☐	4. God and humans share power and responsibility. *(Coauthor, Receptive Resourcers as Co-coaches, Jazz Band Leader, Dance Partner, Intimate and Infinite Friend ...)*
☐	☐	☐	☐	☐	☐	5. God is steady, always there. *(Rock, Best Friend, Divine Companion, Fountain of Living Water, Good-Guy Coach, Ground of Being, Presence, Mighty Fortress, Silent Partner, Holy Breath, Bright Night Light ...)*

I don't think this is true.	This is not *my* experience.	Interesting idea; I might consider it.	I sometimes think this is true.	I often think this way.	This is one of my core beliefs.	
☐	☐	☐	☐	☐	☐	6. God understands and loves us, patiently, tenderly, forever, no matter what. *(Dynamic Love, Mother-Father God, Sister God, Brother God, Grandmother God ...)*
☐	☐	☐	☐	☐	☐	7. God comforts us, protects us. *(Daddy, Abba Mia, Divine Mama, Comforter, Consoler, Shelter from the Storm, Womb of Life, Mother Hen ...)*
☐	☐	☐	☐	☐	☐	8. God takes what is, again and again, and seeks to create the best out of it. *(Choreographer of Chaos, Healer, Improviser, Divine Physical Therapist, Creative-Nurturing God ...)*
☐	☐	☐	☐	☐	☐	9. God encourages us to be the best we can be. *(Attentive Affirmer Coach, Creating Spirit ...)*
☐	☐	☐	☐	☐	☐	10. God knows our limits and works with us to use our potential as fully as we can. *(Divine Physical Therapist, Caregiver ...)*
☐	☐	☐	☐	☐	☐	11. God takes care of us. *(Physician of the Soul, Divine Nurse, Caregiver, Spokesperson God ...)*
☐	☐	☐	☐	☐	☐	12. God catches us or rescues us if we get into trouble. *(Mother Eagle, Rescuer ...)*

I don't think this is true.	This is not *my* experience.	Interesting idea; I might consider it.	I sometimes think this is true.	I often think this way.	This is one of my core beliefs.	
☐	☐	☐	☐	☐	☐	13. God helps us to navigate through difficult waters. *(Compass, Sail, and Wind …)*
☐	☐	☐	☐	☐	☐	14. God gives us strength. *(Nursing Mother God, Persistent Life …)*
☐	☐	☐	☐	☐	☐	15. God watches and assesses our every action. *(Judge, King …)*
☐	☐	☐	☐	☐	☐	16. God wants the best for us, but is not perfect. *(Caregiver over Thirty-Five Accepting Her/His Own Ambiguity …)*
☐	☐	☐	☐	☐	☐	17. God offers wisdom, ideas *(Creative Wisdom, Graffiti Artist, Improviser, Divine Whisper …)*
☐	☐	☐	☐	☐	☐	18. God influences us *and* is influenced by us; God motivates us to interact with each other, to support and empower each other. *(Receptive Resourcers as Co-coaches, Team Transformer Coach, Jazz Band Leader …)*
☐	☐	☐	☐	☐	☐	19. God relates to each of us personally; there are no "one size fits all" responses from God. *(Divine Blacksmith …)*
☐	☐	☐	☐	☐	☐	20. God hovers over us and is there to help. *(Helicopter God, Grandmother God …)*

I don't think this is true.	This is not *my* experience.	Interesting idea; I might consider it.	I sometimes think this is true.	I often think this way.	This is one of my core beliefs.	
☐	☐	☐	☐	☐	☐	21. God created the beautiful earth and everything good in it. *(Creator, Author of Life, Poet of the Universe, Composer)*
☐	☐	☐	☐	☐	☐	22. God is always with us. *(Shekinah, Divine Presence, Infinite Friend, Light, Helicopter God, Uncountable Infinity ...)*
☐	☐	☐	☐	☐	☐	23. God *is. (The Power of Pure Being, Spirit, Breath, Music Itself, Ground of Being, Spiritual Presence, Directing Creativity, Beingness, the Great "I AM," Uncountable Infinity ...)*
☐	☐	☐	☐	☐	☐	24. God improvises. *(Divine Jazz Band Leader, Divine Gardener ...)*

Add your own thoughts, beliefs, and metaphors:

25. ______________________________

26. ______________________________

27. ______________________________

28. ______________________________

29. ______________________________

30. ______________________________

REFLECTIVE QUESTIONS

Introduction

1. What metaphors for God were you taught as a child? What was your image of God then?
2. How have your images and metaphors for God changed over time?
3. Think of three metaphors you use for God today and write them down. Your metaphors might be from your place of worship, your reading, or what you picture when you are crying or smiling in bed at night.
4. Consider what each of these metaphors suggests about what you believe about God, and what each infers about what you hope to experience from or with God.
5. Complete the God Belief Checklist on page 133.
6. If you are meeting with others, get into small groups of three to five people and share what core belief items you have checked. If you are reflecting on this privately, make a list of your core beliefs.

Chapter 1: God the *What*?

1. What metaphors for God (either in scripture or that you've heard other people use) intrigue you? What metaphors trouble you?
2. Select a God metaphor that you are familiar with and explore both sides of it: How do you think God *is* like that? How do you think God is *not* like that?
3. Have you had an experience when a God metaphor that used to "work" for you no longer fits? What changed in your life at that time? How did that affect your metaphor(s) for God?

4. Do any of the six new metaphors suggested in this chapter resonate with you? In what ways?

    - God the Bright Night Light: a God who provides comfort in the dark
    - God the Compass, Sail, and Wind: a God who helps us navigate
    - God the Divine Blacksmith: a God who knows what fits
    - God the Divine Physical Therapist: a God who helps us maximize our potential
    - God the Nursing Mother: a God who cares for me as I care
    - God the Uncountable Infinity: a God who meets my need to be logical

5. Think of a God metaphor that is common in your place of worship. Consider the qualities of God that this metaphor *points to.* See if you can come up with a different metaphor that captures some of the same qualities.
6. Take some time to write your own version of Psalm 23. What metaphor would express, in an ultra-relevant manner, your faith in a comforting and caring God, as Shepherd did for the original psalmist?

Chapter 2: God Can Do *What*? God's Power

1. What is your first response to natural disasters? Where do you see God fitting in the picture?
2. What kinds of encouragement have you heard from people when you have suffered an illness, catastrophe, or loss? How did their words help (or not help)? How did they fit with your beliefs about God?
3. Consider someone who has power in your life. How do they affect you? How do they get you to do something? To *not* do

something? Consider someone who has creative and good power in your life but who does not use any kind of coercive force. How would you describe that power?

4. Think about your favorite hymn, praise song, or worship chant. Consider the words you sing and what they infer about God's power. How similar or dissimilar is this description to the God you believe in?
5. Which of the metaphor(s) described in this chapter come closest to your belief about God's power? Are there any metaphors that you'd like to explore further?

    - God the Almighty: total power
    - God the Post-heroic CEO, God the Tough Love Parent: restrained power
    - God with Us (Helicopter God): the power of presence
    - God *Is* (Spirit, Breath, Ground of Being): the power of pure being
    - Ambiguous God (God the Caregiver over Thirty-Five Accepting Her/His Own Ambiguity): the power of good intentions
    - God as Dynamic Love: the power of love
    - God as Persistent Life: the power of transformation
    - God the Jazz Band Leader: the power of shared power

6. Think of a time in your life when things seemed to be a mess or in chaos. As you look back on that experience, how do you understand God working? What metaphor(s) could you use to describe God's presence or action in this experience?

Chapter 3: God Wants *What*? God's Will

1. How much, or how little, are you a "what is, *is* meant to be" person? Do you believe that everything that *is*, is God's will?
2. Do you think God wants something from humans? If so, how do you think we find clues to understand what God wants?
3. Think of some noes in your life that were important. Describe some of the results of your noes.
4. Think of a time in your life when you improvised. What surprises or good things came of creating in the moment?
5. Do you imagine God more as a Planner or an Improviser? What metaphor(s) might describe your image of God when it comes to this issue of control?
6. Think of a current situation in your life where you (or a family member or close friend) are trying to make an important decision. Make a list of "clues" that seem to suggest one or two possible directions. Would you attribute any of these clues to God? Where and how might you look for other clues? What metaphor would you use to describe God's guidance in this situation?

Chapter 4: God Interacts *How*? Our Relationship with God

1. Name two people you admire and identify some of their qualities that you would like to have or to develop within yourself.
2. Think of two people with whom you like to spend time. What is the "give and take" like in each relationship? How is this important to the quality of your relationship?
3. How do you see yourself as being "like" God in some ways? As being "with" God?
4. How do you think your beliefs about God affect *your* actions? How do your beliefs affect how you view *other* people?

5. Of the five coach metaphors presented in this section, which one(s) most closely match your beliefs about God? How do you see that metaphoric concept of God at work in your life?

    - God the Distant Decider Coach
    - God the Attentive Affirmer Coach
    - God the Good-Guy Coach
    - God the Receptive Resourcers as Co-coaches
    - God the Team Transformer Coach

6. Imagine what it would have been like for you if you had been shown a creative and diverse array of images for God beginning when you were very young. Consider how that would have helped you sense that you (and all others) are in some ways made in the image of God, *and* that you could come to trust that you (and all others) are also *with* God? If you were asked to teach a group of children something about God, what metaphor(s) might you use?

Epilogue: Personal Metaphor Wondering

1. Complete God Metaphor Checklist 1 on page 136.
2. If you are meeting with others, get into small groups of three to five people and share whether anything has shifted since you filled out the God Belief Checklist at the start of the group meetings. (If you are reflecting on this privately, make special note of anything that seems to be shifting in your thinking. Add any notes you wish to the core beliefs list you made at the outset.)
3. Name two to six metaphors for God that feel vital and authentic for you today.
4. What metaphors might help you *relate* to God, as you believe in God?
5. What metaphors might help you *expand* your experience of God?

6. Experiment with writing a prayer using a God metaphor that you like, or take a familiar prayer and change the God metaphor. (If you are meeting with a group, each person could read one of his or her prayers as a way to close the last meeting of the group.)

Invitations for Future Exploration

1. Keep a notebook where you can jot down possible metaphors for God as they occur to you.
2. Start a prayer with a metaphor at random and see how that prayer proceeds. (You might find it helpful to use the Metaphor Index on page 160 for possibilities.)
3. Use the Scripture Index on page 159 to look up various biblical metaphors for God. Note your response (both intellectually and emotionally) to each.
4. Complete God Metaphor Checklist 2 on page 140 after some time has passed (perhaps a year). Compare it to your earlier checklists to see whether anything has changed for you.

DISCUSSION GUIDE FOR GROUPS

The following suggestions are for a group or class who reads this book together. I have arranged them in a six-meeting format. Each meeting includes ideas on how to start the group, how to use the Reflective Questions (which include a written activity for each meeting), as well as a suggested "homework" assignment for the next meeting. I also highly encourage you to open each discussion with a prayer that employs a different metaphor for God. This will be a terrific opportunity to explore a wide variety of God metaphors.

Meeting 1
Opening Reflection on God Metaphors

Leader: Present the ideas from the Introduction.
Use the Introduction questions for group participation and discussion. As a way of modeling for the group, you might describe the metaphors for God you were taught as a child and how you imagined God then.

Activity: Complete the God Belief Checklist. (Go over the directions in the Epilogue on how to use the first checklist.)

Assignment: Read the Introduction and chapter 1: "God the *What*?" for the next gathering.

Meeting 2
Reflection on Chapter 1—God the *What*?

Leader: Use the Reflective Questions for chapter 1 for group participation and discussion. As a way of modeling for the group, you might describe a metaphor for God that used to work for you but no longer seems to fit.

Activity: Write a personal version of Psalm 23, using a different metaphor for God than Shepherd.

Assignment: Read chapter 2: "God Can Do *What*? God's Power" for the next gathering.

Meeting 3
Reflection on Chapter 2—God Can Do *What*? God's Power

Leader: Use the Reflective Questions for chapter 2 for group participation and discussion. As a way to launch the discussion about God's power, you might talk about a natural disaster that has occurred in your area, or a catastrophe that has caught world attention. Use the discussion to segue into the first discussion question, where do you see God fitting in the picture?

Activity: Describe a chaotic time in your life and list some metaphors for God that might describe God's involvement.

Assignment: Read chapter 3: "God Wants *What*? God's Will" for the next gathering.

Meeting 4
Reflection on Chapter 3—God Wants *What*? God's Will

Leader: Use the Reflective Questions for chapter 3 for group participation and discussion. As a way to begin the discussion about God's will, you might want to ask the group to do some "popcorn" brainstorming about the pros and cons of believing that *everything* that happens is God's will. (If possible, have someone write down the group's ideas on a board or newsprint.)

Activity: Make a list of "clues" about an important decision, identifying a possible metaphor for God's guidance in this situation.

Assignment: Read chapter 4: "God Interacts *How*? Our Relationship with God" and the "Conclusion: Metaphors Matter" for the next gathering.

Meeting 5
Reflection on Chapter 4—God Interacts *How*? Our Relationship with God and Conclusion

Leader: Use the Reflective Questions from chapter 4 for group participation and discussion. You might start by naming one person whom you admire and describing how you identify with them. Then describe a person with whom you like to spend time, and how the "give and take" in your relationship is important.

Activity: Write a short vignette using a unique metaphor for God that would describe how God might interact.

Assignment: Write a prayer using this metaphor for God.

Meeting 6
Reflection on the Epilogue—Epilogue: Personal Metaphor Wondering

Leader: Go over the directions for completing the God Metaphor Checklist. Then proceed with the Epilogue questions.

Activity: Complete God Metaphor Checklist 1.

Assignment: Consider the Invitations for Future Exploration on page 149, which include revisiting the God Metaphor Checklist at a later date to see if anything has changed.

NOTES

Introduction

1. Carolyn Stahl Bohler, *Prayer on Wings: A Search for Authentic Prayer* (San Diego: LuraMedia, 1990).
2. *The 72 Names of God* (Los Angeles: Kabbalah Publishing Company, 2004) is available in two forms: a book subtitled *The Course: Technology for the Soul* and a meditation deck of cards.

Chapter 1: God the *What*?

1. Biblical scholars describe four major theological viewpoints evident in the Hebrew Bible. They name these sources "J," "E," "P," and "D"—Jahwist, Elohist, Priestly, and Deuteronomist. The Deuteronomist also refers to God as YHWH. In the Elohist material, God is Elohim (until Exod. 3), and God speaks in dreams. God is also Elohim (until Exod. 3) in the Priestly material, which includes long genealogies and majestic speeches about God. "Documentary Hypothesis," http://ccat.sas.upenn.edu/rs/2/Judaism/jepd.html.
2. Sallie McFague's discussion in *Metaphorical Theology: Models of God in Religious Language* (Philadelphia: Fortress Press, 1982) of metaphors in general, and metaphors for God in particular, remains for me the best explanation of the use of metaphors for God. She explains that a metaphor needs to be relevant, as I have said here, but also that it cannot be idolatrous, that is, identified as God. Sometimes we use a metaphor so often that we begin to think of that metaphor *as* God, not as a metaphor. If that happens, it has become an idol. A metaphor only functions as it is supposed to—to get us to think of God—if it is both relevant and not idolatrous.
3. Carl Sandburg, "Fog": "The fog comes / on little cat feet."
4. Dr. Carl Stanley, "Beside Still Waters," *Saturday Evening Post*, December 1974.
5. Toki Miyashina, "The 23rd Psalm for Busy People," in *Psalm 23: Several Versions Collected and Put Together*, ed. K. H. Strange (Edinburgh: St. Andrew Press, 1969).

6. John A. T. Robinson, *Honest to God* (Philadelphia: The Westminster Press, 1963).
7. Suzanne Fisher Staples, *Shabanu: Daughter of the Wind* (New York: Random House, 1991).
8. In *Battered Love: Marriage, Sex, and Violence in the Hebrew Prophets* (Minneapolis: Fortress Press, 1995), Renita J. Weems discusses the abusive husband images of God in Hosea 2:1–13; Jeremiah 2:1–3, 13:20–27; and Ezekiel 16:24, showing the political situation at the time that led to this metaphor for God that was intended to insult the listeners.
9. These similes are several of the ones named in my children's book, *God Is Like a Mother Hen and Much Much More* (Louisville, Ky.: Presbyterian Publishing Corporation, 1996), in which I ask the reader to think of what God is like.
10. Mary Daly's *Beyond God the Father: Toward a Philosophy of Women's Liberation* (Boston: Beacon Press, 1973) set the stage for many writers and thinkers to reflect upon viable ways to think of God.
11. Since I first wrote these thoughts, the Women's National Basketball Association has been created, so this limitation, for *some* especially athletic 5'3" females, may be removed.
12. Some have found this mathematical musing on God and humans more comprehensible by considering a one-dimensional line, infinitely long; a two-dimensional plane, such as an infinitely expansive sheet of paper; and a three-dimensional box that can expand in all of its directions. We can consider humans to be like infinitely long lines, always able to expand and grow, but having certain limits in direction and width. Then we could consider God to be like the three-dimensional box that includes lines in every possible direction. (If you think of God like the infinite box, then you could consider human communities to be like a two-dimensional plane.) The point is that both humans and God are infinite, but humans have limits while we are infinite, and God is both limitless (or at least has far fewer limits than a human has) and is infinite.
13. Theologically, this model is described as "panentheistic," for God is both within all *and* beyond all. Panentheism is neither pantheism (God is in whatever is), nor theism (God is beyond what we see).

Chapter 2: God Can Do *What*? God's Power

1. In *Journey Through the Bible: Job, Psalms, Proverbs* (Nashville, Tenn.: Cokesbury, 1995), p. 7, Kathy Farmer explains that the understanding

of Satan has gone through phases and has developed just as views of God have. Centuries before Christ, there was not a belief in Satan as an evil being. That view developed later. At the time of Job, "the satan" was thought to be just one of the angels in heaven whose function it was to act as "the prosecuting attorney" in a mock legal trial that was set in heaven.

2. Farmer, *Journey Through the Bible,* 3.
3. I heard this phrase used on National Public Radio by a relief worker for tsunami victims, to describe himself as he received aid and tried to organize sending it out to those who needed it. He called himself a "choreographer of chaos."
4. Thornton Wilder, *The Bridge of San Luis Rey* (New York: HarperCollins, 1927), 5.
5. Ibid., 5.
6. Ibid., 6.
7. Ibid., 113.
8. Ibid., 113.
9. Ibid., 111.
10. Marjorie Hewett Suchocki, *In God's Presence: Theological Reflections on Prayer* (St. Louis: Chalice Press, 1996), 16.
11. Dr. Henry Mitchell, prominent preacher, teacher, and author, in oral discussion, March 18, 1997.
12. Malcolm Boyd, *Are You Running with Me, Jesus?* (New York: Holt, Rinehart and Winston, 1965; Lanham, Md.: Cowley Publications, 2006).
13. Paul Tillich spoke of God as "Spiritual Presence" and the "Ground of Being." In his *Systematic Theology: Three Volumes in One* (Chicago: University of Chicago Press, 1967), he wrote of the guidance God provides as "directing creativity."
14. Process theologian Henry N. Wieman wrote of God in a manner that leads nicely to the metaphor Source of Creative Good in *The Source of Human Good* (London: Edwardsville Feffer & Simons, 1946; Eugene, Ore.: Wipf & Stock Publishers, 2008).
15. In chapter 8 of *The Abuse of Power: A Theological Problem* (Nashville, Tenn.: Abingdon, 1991), James Newton Poling compassionately discusses the possibility of God's ambivalence amid a description of the "search for God" by those who have abused or have been abused.
16. Wilder, 123.
17. Ibid., 123.

Chapter 3: God Wants *What*? God's Will

1. I wrote an earlier version of this first section as a church newsletter column for Aldersgate United Methodist Church, where I served as pastor, on October 8, 2003, two days before our son died.
2. All the information shared here is from the *Los Angeles Times,* July 30, 2006, E38.
3. Suchocki, *In God's Presence,* 18–19.
4. Belshazzar was in charge only temporarily. He was not really the king; he was filling in for his dad.

Chapter 4: God Interacts *How*? Our Relationship with God

1. Jerome Kagan, *The Nature of the Child* (New York: Basic Books, 1984).
2. The events of the Christian liturgical year reiterate again and again that we are *with* God. During Advent, Christians celebrate the coming of God into the world to be with us in the presence of Christ. Jesus is born and called Immanuel, which means literally, "God is with us." Jesus's predominant message throughout his ministry was precisely that: God is here now; the Kingdom of God is at hand. The coming of the wise ones to the Christ in Bethlehem is celebrated with Epiphany, which means "God appears, is manifested, is with us." The Resurrection celebrates the restoring of relationship with God, through the risen Christ. Even Pentecost focuses on affiliation as it celebrates the presence of the Holy Spirit with the community of faith.
3. In *The Birth of the Living God: A Psychoanalytic Study* (Chicago: University of Chicago Press, 1979), Ana-Maria Rizzuto discusses the internal representation of God and how it develops, using an object relations psychoanalytic approach.
4. Frederich Schleiermacher, *Selected Sermons* (New York: Frank and Wagnalls, n.d.), 36–51. Also, Schleiermacher, *The Christian Faith* (Philadelphia: Fortress, 1928), 226, 673–74.
5. Sam Register, article in *Newsweek,* July 19, 1999, 50–54.
6. Ibid., 50–54.
7. When Kushner wrote *When Bad Things Happen to Good People* (New York: Avon, 1981), he had not considered power as other than a forceful power that makes things happen. Kushner was later introduced to the process theology notion of God having persuasive power. This idea may have altered Kushner's position regarding God's limiting

God's own power. See the video *Human Suffering and the Power of God,* an interview of Harold Kushner by John Cobb, School of Theology at Claremont, 1986.

8. Bernard M. Loomer, "Two Kinds of Power," *Criterion* (Winter 1976): 13–20 passim.
9. Ibid., 13–20.
10. Ibid., 13–20.
11. Ibid., 13–20.
12. Gordon E. Jackson, *Pastoral Care and Process Theology* (Washington, D.C.: University Press of America, 1981).
13. Register, article in *Newsweek,* 50–54.
14. Mia Hamm, the highest-scoring woman in the history of international soccer sees herself as a "solid cog in a remarkably powerful machine. 'People do not want to hear that I'm no better than my teammates ... but I'm not. Everything I am I owe to this team.'" Ibid., 53.
15. "Multiple-Choice God: New Survey Reveals That Americans Believe in Four Basic Types of Deity," *Los Angeles Times,* September 17, 2006, M4.
16. Ibid., M4.
17. Ibid., M4.
18. Ibid., M4.
19. Ibid., M4.
20. Ibid., M4.

CREDITS

Scripture quotations, unless otherwise marked, are from the New Revised Standard Version Bible, copyright © 1989 by the Division of Christian Education of the National Council of the Churches of Christ in the USA. Used by permission. All rights reserved.

Translation of the Qur'an is taken from *The Holy Qur'an: Original Arabic Text with English Translation & Selected Commentaries*, by 'Abdullah Yusuf Ali (Kuala Lumpur, Malaysia: Saba Islamic Media, 2000). Ali's translation is also widely available online.

Some parts of this book originally appeared in slightly different form in the following publications:

"God as Jazz Band Leader: Divine and Human Power and Responsibility," *Journal of Theology* (Summer 1997).

"God Is Like a Jazz Band Leader: Location of Divine and Human Power and Responsibility—A Call to Pastoral Theologians," *Journal of Pastoral Theology* (Summer 1997): 23–42.

"God the Uncountable Infinity" (chapter 1) was originally published as "Varieties of Religious Infinities," In *The Christian Century,* January 16, 1991, 38–39.

"In Search of a Defense Mechanism? In Search of God?" *Journal of Pastoral Care* 50, no. 3 (Fall 1996). Reprinted in *Journeys,* published by American Association of Pastoral Counselors, 2002.

"Coaches and Gods," *Journal of Pastoral Theology* 14, no. 1 (Spring 2004): 15–30.

All the vignettes in this book evolved from real individuals or composites of the experiences of several people. No example is fabricated or merely theoretical. However, all names in the vignettes are fictitious.

HEBREW, CHRISTIAN, AND ISLAMIC SCRIPTURES INDEX

METAPHOR INDEX

AVAILABLE FROM BETTER BOOKSTORES.
TRY YOUR BOOKSTORE FIRST.

Inspiration

The Rebirthing of God
Christianity's Struggle for New Beginnings
By John Philip Newell
Drawing on modern prophets from East and West, and using the holy island of Iona as an icon of new beginnings, Celtic poet, peacemaker and scholar John Philip Newell dares us to imagine a new birth from deep within Christianity, a fresh stirring of the Spirit.
6 x 9, 160 pp, HC, 978-1-59473-542-4 **$19.99**

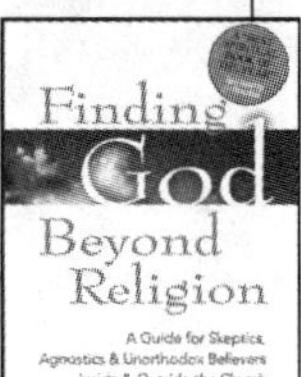

Finding God Beyond Religion: A Guide for Skeptics, Agnostics & Unorthodox Believers Inside & Outside the Church
By Tom Stella; Foreword by The Rev. Canon Marianne Wells Borg
Reinterprets traditional religious teachings central to the Christian faith for people who have outgrown the beliefs and devotional practices that once made sense to them.
6 x 9, 160 pp, Quality PB, 978-1-59473-485-4 **$16.99**

Fully Awake and Truly Alive: Spiritual Practices to Nurture Your Soul
By Rev. Jane E. Vennard; Foreword by Rami Shapiro
Illustrates the joys and frustrations of spiritual practice, offers insights from various religious traditions and provides exercises and meditations to help us become more fully alive.
6 x 9, 208 pp, Quality PB, 978-1-59473-473-1 **$16.99**

Journeys of Simplicity: Traveling Light with Thomas Merton, Bashō, Edward Abbey, Annie Dillard & Others *By Philip Harnden*
Invites you to consider a more graceful way of traveling through life. Includes journal pages to help you get started on your own spiritual journey.
5 x 7¼, 144 pp, Quality PB, 978-1-59473-181-5 **$12.99**

Perennial Wisdom for the Spiritually Independent
Sacred Teachings—Annotated & Explained
Annotation by Rami Shapiro; Foreword by Richard Rohr
Weaves sacred texts and teachings from the world's major religions into a coherent exploration of the five core questions at the heart of every religion's search.
5½ x 8½, 336 pp, Quality PB, 978-1-59473-515-8 **$16.99**

Saving Civility: 52 Ways to Tame Rude, Crude & Attitude for a Polite Planet
By Sara Hacala
Provides fifty-two practical ways you can reverse the course of incivility and make the world a more enriching, pleasant place to live.
6 x 9, 240 pp, Quality PB, 978-1-59473-314-7 **$16.99**

Spiritually Healthy Divorce: Navigating Disruption with Insight & Hope
By Carolyne Call
A spiritual map to help you move through the twists and turns of divorce.
6 x 9, 224 pp, Quality PB, 978-1-59473-288-1 **$16.99**

Or phone, fax, mail or email to: SKYLIGHT PATHS **Publishing**
Sunset Farm Offices, Route 4 • P.O. Box 237 • Woodstock, Vermont 05091
Tel: (802) 457-4000 • Fax: (802) 457-4004 • www.skylightpaths.com
Credit card orders: (800) 962-4544 (8:30AM–5:30PM EST Monday–Friday)
Generous discounts on quantity orders. SATISFACTION GUARANTEED. Prices subject to change.

Bible Stories / Folktales

Abraham's Bind & Other Bible Tales of Trickery, Folly, Mercy and Love *By Michael J. Caduto*
New retellings of episodes in the lives of familiar biblical characters explore relevant life lessons. 6 x 9, 224 pp, HC, 978-1-59473-186-0 **$19.99**

Daughters of the Desert: Stories of Remarkable Women from Christian, Jewish and Muslim Traditions *By Claire Rudolf Murphy, Meghan Nuttall Sayres, Mary Cronk Farrell, Sarah Conover and Betsy Wharton*
Breathes new life into the old tales of our female ancestors in faith. Uses traditional scriptural passages as starting points, then with vivid detail fills in historical context and place. Chapters reveal the voices of Sarah, Hagar, Huldah, Esther, Salome, Mary Magdalene, Lydia, Khadija, Fatima and many more. Historical fiction ideal for readers of all ages.
5½ x 8½, 192 pp, Quality PB, 978-1-59473-106-8 **$18.99** Inc. reader's discussion guide

The Triumph of Eve & Other Subversive Bible Tales
By Matt Biers-Ariel
These engaging retellings of familiar Bible stories are witty, often hilarious and always profound. They invite you to grapple with questions and issues that are often hidden in the original texts.
5½ x 8½, 192 pp, Quality PB, 978-1-59473-176-1 **$14.99**

Also available: **The Triumph of Eve Teacher's Guide**
8½ x 11, 44 pp, PB, 978-1-59473-152-5 **$8.99**

Wisdom in the Telling
Finding Inspiration and Grace in Traditional Folktales and Myths Retold
By Lorraine Hartin-Gelardi
6 x 9, 192 pp, HC, 978-1-59473-185-3 **$19.99**

Religious Etiquette / Reference

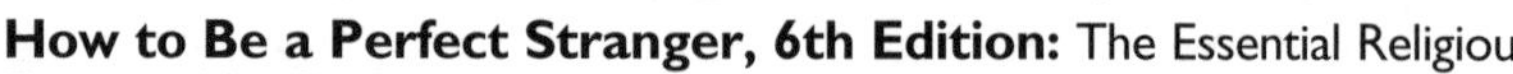

How to Be a Perfect Stranger, 6th Edition: The Essential Religious Etiquette Handbook *Edited by Stuart M. Matlins and Arthur J. Magida*
The indispensable guidebook to help the well-meaning guest when visiting other people's religious ceremonies. A straightforward guide to the rituals and celebrations of the major religions and denominations in the United States and Canada from the perspective of an interested guest of any other faith, based on information obtained from authorities of each religion. Belongs in every living room, library and office. Covers:
African American Methodist Churches • Assemblies of God • Bahá'í Faith • Baptist • Buddhist • Christian Church (Disciples of Christ) • Christian Science (Church of Christ, Scientist) • Churches of Christ • Episcopalian and Anglican • Hindu • Islam • Jehovah's Witnesses • Jewish • Lutheran • Mennonite/Amish • Methodist • Mormon (Church of Jesus Christ of Latter-day Saints) • Native American/First Nations • Orthodox Churches • Pentecostal Church of God • Presbyterian • Quaker (Religious Society of Friends) • Reformed Church in America/Canada • Roman Catholic • Seventh-day Adventist • Sikh • Unitarian Universalist • United Church of Canada • United Church of Christ

"The things Miss Manners forgot to tell us about religion."
—*Los Angeles Times*

"Finally, for those inclined to undertake their own spiritual journeys … tells visitors what to expect." —*New York Times*

6 x 9, 432 pp, Quality PB, 978-1-59473-593-6 **$19.99**

The Perfect Stranger's Guide to Funerals and Grieving Practices
A Guide to Etiquette in Other People's Religious Ceremonies
Edited by Stuart M. Matlins 6 x 9, 240 pp, Quality PB, 978-1-893361-20-1 **$16.95**

The Perfect Stranger's Guide to Wedding Ceremonies
A Guide to Etiquette in Other People's Religious Ceremonies
Edited by Stuart M. Matlins 6 x 9, 208 pp, Quality PB, 978-1-893361-19-5 **$16.95**

Judaism / Christianity / Islam / Interfaith

Practical Interfaith: How to Find Our Common Humanity as We Celebrate Diversity
By Rev. Steven Greenebaum
Explores Interfaith as a faith—and as a positive way to move forward. Offers a practical, down-to-earth approach to a more spiritually fulfilling life.
6 x 9, 176 pp, Quality PB, 978-1-59473-569-1 **$16.99**

Sacred Laughter of the Sufis: Awakening the Soul with the Mulla's Comic Teaching Stories & Other Islamic Wisdom
By Imam Jamal Rahman
The legendary wisdom stories of the Mulla, Islam's great comic foil, with spiritual insights for seekers of all traditions—or none.
6 x 9, 192 pp, Quality PB, 978-1-59473-547-9 **$16.99**

Spiritual Gems of Islam: Insights & Practices from the Qur'an, Hadith, Rumi & Muslim Teaching Stories to Enlighten the Heart & Mind
By Imam Jamal Rahman
Invites you—no matter what your practice may be—to access the treasure chest of Islamic spirituality and use its wealth in your own journey.
6 x 9, 256 pp, Quality PB, 978-1-59473-430-4 **$16.99**

Religion Gone Astray: What We Found at the Heart of Interfaith
By Pastor Don Mackenzie, Rabbi Ted Falcon and Imam Jamal Rahman
Welcome to the deeper dimensions of interfaith dialogue—exploring that which divides us personally, spiritually and institutionally.
6 x 9, 192 pp, Quality PB, 978-1-59473-317-8 **$16.99**

Blessed Relief: What Christians Can Learn from Buddhists about Suffering
By Gordon Peerman 6 x 9, 208 pp, Quality PB, 978-1-59473-252-2 **$16.99**

Christians & Jews—Faith to Faith: Tragic History, Promising Present, Fragile Future *By Rabbi James Rudin*
6 x 9, 288 pp, HC, 978-1-58023-432-0 **$24.99**; Quality PB, 978-1-58023-717-8 **$18.99***

Christians & Jews in Dialogue: Learning in the Presence of the Other
By Mary C. Boys and Sara S. Lee; Foreword by Dorothy C. Bass
6 x 9, 240 pp, Quality PB, 978-1-59473-254-6 **$18.99**

Getting to the Heart of Interfaith: The Eye-Opening, Hope-Filled Friendship of a Pastor, a Rabbi & an Imam *By Pastor Don Mackenzie, Rabbi Ted Falcon and Imam Jamal Rahman*
6 x 9, 192 pp, Quality PB, 978-1-59473-263-8 **$16.99**

Hearing the Call across Traditions: Readings on Faith and Service
Edited by Adam Davis; Foreword by Eboo Patel
6 x 9, 352 pp, Quality PB, 978-1-59473-303-1 **$18.99**

InterActive Faith: The Essential Interreligious Community-Building Handbook
Edited by Rev. Bud Heckman with Rori Picker Neiss; Foreword by Rev. Dirk Ficca
6 x 9, 304 pp, Quality PB, 978-1-59473-273-7 **$16.99**; HC, 978-1-59473-237-9 **$29.99**

The Jewish Approach to God: A Brief Introduction for Christians
By Rabbi Neil Gillman, PhD 5½ x 8½, 192 pp, Quality PB, 978-1-58023-190-9 **$16.95***

The Jewish Approach to Repairing the World (*Tikkun Olam*)
A Brief Introduction for Christians *By Rabbi Elliot N. Dorff, PhD, with Rev. Cory Willson*
5½ x 8½, 256 pp, Quality PB, 978-1-58023-349-1 **$16.99***

The Jewish Connection to Israel, the Promised Land: A Brief Introduction for Christians *By Rabbi Eugene Korn, PhD* 5½ x 8½, 192 pp, Quality PB, 978-1-58023-318-7 **$14.99***

Jewish Holidays: A Brief Introduction for Christians *By Rabbi Kerry M. Olitzky and Rabbi Daniel Judson* 5½ x 8½, 176 pp, Quality PB, 978-1-58023-302-6 **$18.99***

Jewish Ritual: A Brief Introduction for Christians *By Rabbi Kerry M. Olitzky and Rabbi Daniel Judson* 5½ x 8½, 144 pp, Quality PB, 978-1-58023-210-4 **$14.99***

Jewish Spirituality: A Brief Introduction for Christians
By Rabbi Lawrence Kushner 5½ x 8½, 112 pp, Quality PB, 978-1-58023-150-3 **$12.95***

*A book from Jewish Lights, SkyLight Paths' sister imprint

Sacred Texts—SkyLight Illuminations Series

Offers today's spiritual seeker an enjoyable entry into the great classic texts of the world's spiritual traditions. Each classic is presented in an accessible translation, with facing pages of guided commentary from experts, giving you the keys you need to understand the history, context and meaning of the text.

CHRISTIANITY

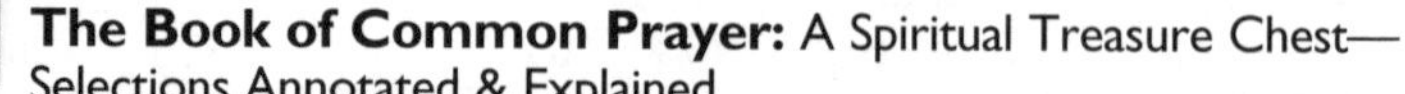

The Book of Common Prayer: A Spiritual Treasure Chest—Selections Annotated & Explained
Annotation by The Rev. Canon C. K. Robertson, PhD; Foreword by The Most Rev. Katharine Jefferts Schori; Preface by Archbishop Desmond Tutu

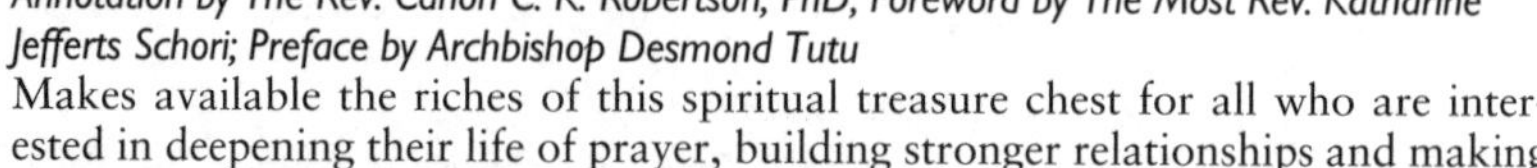

Makes available the riches of this spiritual treasure chest for all who are interested in deepening their life of prayer, building stronger relationships and making a difference in their world. 5½ x 8½, 208 pp, Quality PB, 978-1-59473-524-0 **$16.99**

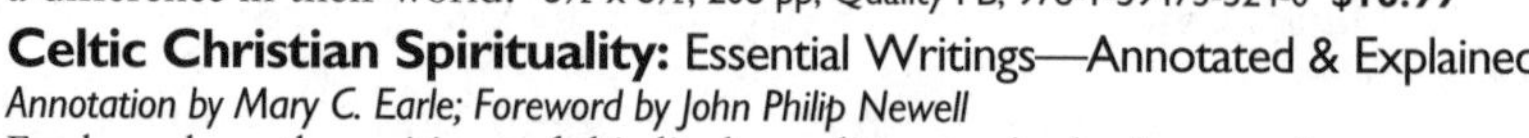

Celtic Christian Spirituality: Essential Writings—Annotated & Explained
Annotation by Mary C. Earle; Foreword by John Philip Newell
Explores how the writings of this lively tradition embody the gospel.
5½ x 8½, 176 pp, Quality PB, 978-1-59473-302-4 **$16.99**

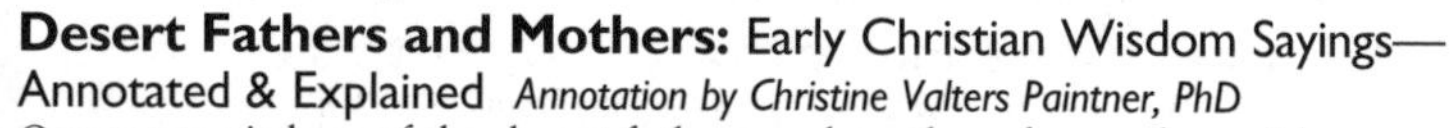

Desert Fathers and Mothers: Early Christian Wisdom Sayings—Annotated & Explained *Annotation by Christine Valters Paintner, PhD*
Opens up wisdom of the desert fathers and mothers for readers with no previous knowledge of Western monasticism and early Christianity.
5½ x 8½, 192 pp, Quality PB, 978-1-59473-373-4 **$16.99**

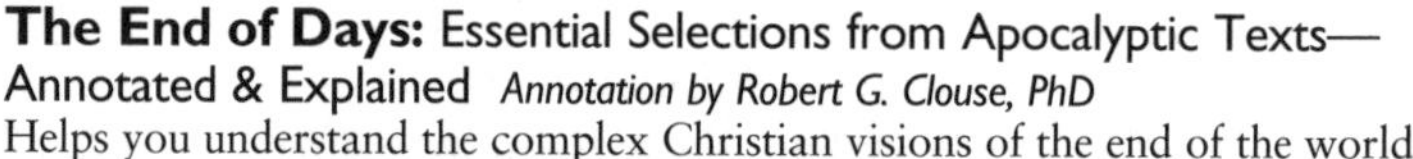

The End of Days: Essential Selections from Apocalyptic Texts—Annotated & Explained *Annotation by Robert G. Clouse, PhD*
Helps you understand the complex Christian visions of the end of the world.
5½ x 8½, 224 pp, Quality PB, 978-1-59473-170-9 **$16.99**

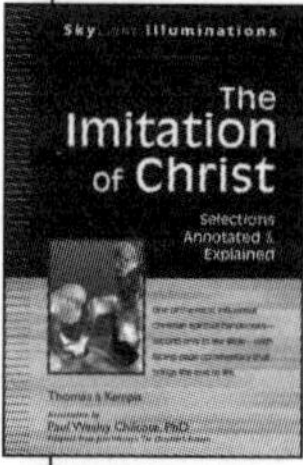

The Hidden Gospel of Matthew: Annotated & Explained
Translation & Annotation by Ron Miller
Discover the words and events that have the strongest connection to the historical Jesus.
5½ x 8½, 272 pp, Quality PB, 978-1-59473-038-2 **$16.99**

The Imitation of Christ: Selections Annotated & Explained
Annotation by Paul Wesley Chilcote, PhD; By Thomas à Kempis; Adapted from John Wesley's The Christian's Pattern
Let Jesus's example of holiness, humility and purity of heart be a companion on your own spiritual journey.
5½ x 8½, 224 pp, Quality PB, 978-1-59473-434-2 **$16.99**

The Infancy Gospels of Jesus: Apocryphal Tales from the Childhoods of Mary and Jesus—Annotated & Explained
Translation & Annotation by Stevan Davies; Foreword by A. Edward Siecienski, PhD
A startling presentation of the early lives of Mary, Jesus and other biblical figures that will amuse and surprise you. 5½ x 8½, 176 pp, Quality PB, 978-1-59473-258-4 **$16.99**

John & Charles Wesley: Selections from Their Writings and Hymns—Annotated & Explained *Annotation by Paul W. Chilcote, PhD*
A unique presentation of the writings of these two inspiring brothers brings together some of the most essential material from their large corpus of work.
5½ x 8½, 288 pp, Quality PB, 978-1-59473-309-3 **$16.99**

Julian of Norwich: Selections from *Revelations of Divine Love*—Annotated & Explained *Annotation by Mary C. Earle; Foreword by Roberta C. Bondi*
Addresses topics including the infinite nature of God, the life of prayer, God's suffering with us, the eternal and undying life of the soul, the motherhood of Jesus and the motherhood of God and more.
5½ x 8½, 224 pp, Quality PB, 978-1-59473-513-4 **$16.99**

Sacred Texts—continued

JUDAISM

The Book of Job: Annotated & Explained
Translation and Annotation by Donald Kraus; Foreword by Dr. Marc Brettler
Clarifies for today's readers what Job is, how to overcome difficulties in the text, and what it may mean for us. 5½ x 8½, 256 pp, Quality PB, 978-1-59473-389-5 **$16.99**

The Divine Feminine in Biblical Wisdom Literature
Selections Annotated & Explained
Translation & Annotation by Rabbi Rami Shapiro; Foreword by Rev. Cynthia Bourgeault, PhD
Uses the Hebrew Bible and Wisdom literature to explain Sophia's way of wisdom and illustrate Her creative energy. 5½ x 8½, 240 pp, Quality PB, 978-1-59473-109-9 **$18.99**

Ecclesiastes: Annotated & Explained
Translation & Annotation by Rabbi Rami Shapiro; Foreword by Rev. Barbara Cawthorne Crafton
A timeless teaching on living well amid uncertainty and insecurity.
5½ x 8½, 160 pp, Quality PB, 978-1-59473-287-4 **$16.99**

Embracing the Divine Feminine: Finding God through the Ecstasy of Physical Love—The Song of Songs Annotated & Explained
Translation & Annotation by Rabbi Rami Shapiro; Foreword by Rev. Cynthia Bourgeault, PhD
Restores the Song of Songs' eroticism and interprets it as a celebration of the love between the Divine Feminine and the contemporary spiritual seeker.
5½ x 8½, 176 pp, Quality PB, 978-1-59473-575-2 **$16.99**

Ethics of the Sages: *Pirke Avot*—Annotated & Explained
Translation & Annotation by Rabbi Rami Shapiro Clarifies the ethical teachings of the early Rabbis. 5½ x 8½, 192 pp, Quality PB, 978-1-59473-207-2 **$16.99**

Hasidic Tales: Annotated & Explained
Translation & Annotation by Rabbi Rami Shapiro; Foreword by Andrew Harvey
Introduces the legendary tales of the impassioned Hasidic rabbis, presenting them as stories rather than as parables. 5½ x 8½, 240 pp, Quality PB, 978-1-893361-86-7 **$18.99**

The Hebrew Prophets: Selections Annotated & Explained
Translation & Annotation by Rabbi Rami Shapiro
Foreword by Rabbi Zalman M. Schachter-Shalomi (z"l) Makes the wisdom of these timeless teachers available to readers with no previous knowledge of the prophets.
5½ x 8½, 224 pp, Quality PB, 978-1-59473-037-5 **$16.99**

Maimonides—Essential Teachings on Jewish Faith & Ethics
The Book of Knowledge & the Thirteen Principles of Faith—Annotated & Explained
Translation and Annotation by Rabbi Marc D. Angel, PhD
Opens up for us Maimonides's views on the nature of God, providence, prophecy, free will, human nature, repentance and more. 5½ x 8½, 224 pp, Quality PB, 978-1-59473-311-6 **$18.99**

Proverbs: Annotated & Explained
Translation and Annotation by Rabbi Rami Shapiro
Demonstrates how these complex poetic forms are actually straightforward instructions to live simply, without rationalizations and excuses.
5½ x 8½, 288 pp, Quality PB, 978-1-59473-310-9 **$16.99**

***Tanya,* the Masterpiece of Hasidic Wisdom**
Selections Annotated & Explained *Translation & Annotation by Rabbi Rami Shapiro*
Foreword by Rabbi Zalman M. Schachter-Shalomi (z"l)
Clarifies one of the most powerful and potentially transformative books of Jewish wisdom. 5½ x 8½, 240 pp, Quality PB, 978-1-59473-275-1 **$18.99**

Zohar: Annotated & Explained
Translation & Annotation by Daniel C. Matt; Foreword by Andrew Harvey
The canonical text of Jewish mystical tradition.
5½ x 8½, 176 pp, Quality PB, 978-1-893361-51-5 **$18.99**

See Inspiration for *Perennial Wisdom for the Spiritually Independent: Sacred Teachings—Annotated & Explained*

Sacred Texts—continued

ISLAM

Ghazali on the Principles of Islamic Spirituality
Selections from *The Forty Foundations of Religion*—Annotated & Explained
Translation & Annotation by Aaron Spevack, PhD; Foreword by M. Fethullah Gülen
Makes the core message of this influential spiritual master relevant to anyone seeking a balanced understanding of Islam.
5½ x 8½, 336 pp, Quality PB, 978-1-59473-284-3 **$18.99**

The Qur'an and Sayings of Prophet Muhammad
Selections Annotated & Explained
Annotation by Sohaib N. Sultan; Translation by Yusuf Ali, Revised by Sohaib N. Sultan
Foreword by Jane I. Smith
Presents the foundational wisdom of Islam in an easy-to-use format.
5½ x 8½, 256 pp, Quality PB, 978-1-59473-222-5 **$16.99**

Rumi and Islam: Selections from His Stories, Poems, and Discourses—Annotated & Explained *Translation & Annotation by Ibrahim Gamard*
Focuses on Rumi's place within the Sufi tradition of Islam, providing insight into the mystical side of the religion. 5½ x 8½, 240 pp, Quality PB, 978-1-59473-002-3 **$18.99**

See Inspiration for *Perennial Wisdom for the Spiritually Independent: Sacred Teachings—Annotated & Explained*

EASTERN RELIGIONS

The Art of War—Spirituality for Conflict: Annotated & Explained
By Sun Tzu; Annotation by Thomas Huynh; Translation by Thomas Huynh and the Editors at Sonshi.com; Foreword by Marc Benioff; Preface by Thomas Cleary
Highlights principles that encourage a perceptive and spiritual approach to conflict.
5½ x 8½, 256 pp, Quality PB, 978-1-59473-244-7 **$16.99**

Bhagavad Gita: Annotated & Explained
Translation by Shri Purohit Swami; Annotation by Kendra Crossen Burroughs
Foreword by Andrew Harvey Presents the classic text's teachings—with no previous knowledge of Hinduism required. 5½ x 8½, 192 pp, Quality PB, 978-1-893361-28-7 **$18.99**

Chuang-tzu: The Tao of Perfect Happiness—Selections Annotated & Explained
Translation & Annotation by Livia Kohn, PhD
Presents Taoism's central message of reverence for the "Way" of the natural world.
5½ x 8½, 240 pp, Quality PB, 978-1-59473-296-6 **$16.99**

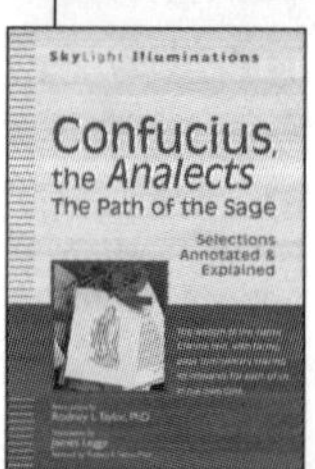

Confucius, the *Analects:* The Path of the Sage—Selections Annotated & Explained *Annotation by Rodney L. Taylor, PhD; Translation by James Legge, Revised by Rodney L. Taylor, PhD* Explores the ethical and spiritual meaning behind the Confucian way of learning and self-cultivation.
5½ x 8½, 192 pp, Quality PB, 978-1-59473-306-2 **$16.99**

Dhammapada: Annotated & Explained
Translation by Max Müller, Revised by Jack Maguire; Annotation by Jack Maguire
Foreword by Andrew Harvey Contains all of Buddhism's key teachings, plus commentary that explains all the names, terms and references.
5½ x 8½, 160 pp, b/w photos, Quality PB, 978-1-893361-42-3 **$14.95**

Selections from the Gospel of Sri Ramakrishna: Annotated & Explained
Translation by Swami Nikhilananda; Annotation by Kendra Crossen Burroughs
Foreword by Andrew Harvey Introduces the fascinating world of the Indian mystic and the universal appeal of his message. 5½ x 8½, 240 pp, b/w photos, Quality PB, 978-1-893361-46-1 **$16.95**

Tao Te Ching: Annotated & Explained
Translation & Annotation by Derek Lin; Foreword by Lama Surya Das
Introduces an Eastern classic in an accessible, poetic and completely original way.
5½ x 8½, 208 pp, Quality PB, 978-1-59473-204-1 **$16.99**

Spiritual Practice—The Sacred Art of Living Series

Dreaming—The Sacred Art: Incubating, Navigating & Interpreting Sacred Dreams for Spiritual & Personal Growth
By Lori Joan Swick, PhD
This fascinating introduction to sacred dreams celebrates the dream experience as a way to deepen spiritual awareness and as a source of self-healing. Designed for the novice and the experienced sacred dreamer of all faith traditions, or none.
5½ x 8½, 224 pp, Quality PB, 978-1-59473-544-8 **$16.99**

Conversation—The Sacred Art: Practicing Presence in an Age of Distraction
By Diane M. Millis, PhD; Foreword by Rev. Tilden Edwards, PhD
5½ x 8½, 192 pp, Quality PB, 978-1-59473-474-8 **$16.99**

Dance—The Sacred Art: The Joy of Movement as a Spiritual Practice
By Cynthia Winton-Henry 5½ x 8½, 224 pp, Quality PB, 978-1-59473-268-3 **$16.99**

Fly-Fishing—The Sacred Art: Casting a Fly as a Spiritual Practice
By Rabbi Eric Eisenkramer and Rev. Michael Attas, MD; Foreword by Chris Wood, CEO, Trout Unlimited; Preface by Lori Simon, executive director, Casting for Recovery
5½ x 8½, 160 pp, Quality PB, 978-1-59473-299-7 **$16.99**

Giving—The Sacred Art: Creating a Lifestyle of Generosity
By Lauren Tyler Wright 5½ x 8½, 208 pp, Quality PB, 978-1-59473-224-9 **$16.99**

Haiku—The Sacred Art: A Spiritual Practice in Three Lines
By Margaret D. McGee 5½ x 8½, 192 pp, Quality PB, 978-1-59473-269-0 **$16.99**

Hospitality—The Sacred Art: Discovering the Hidden Spiritual Power of Invitation and Welcome *By Rev. Nanette Sawyer; Foreword by Rev. Dirk Ficca*
5½ x 8½, 208 pp, Quality PB, 978-1-59473-228-7 **$16.99**

Labyrinths from the Outside In, 2nd Edition
Walking to Spiritual Insight—A Beginner's Guide *By Rev. Dr. Donna Schaper and Rev. Dr. Carole Ann Camp* 6 x 9, 208 pp, b/w illus. and photos, Quality PB, 978-1-59473-486-1 **$16.99**

***Lectio Divina*—The Sacred Art**
Transforming Words & Images into Heart-Centered Prayer
By Christine Valters Paintner, PhD 5½ x 8½, 240 pp, Quality PB, 978-1-59473-300-0 **$16.99**

Pilgrimage—The Sacred Art: Journey to the Center of the Heart
By Dr. Sheryl A. Kujawa-Holbrook 5½ x 8½, 240 pp, Quality PB, 978-1-59473-472-4 **$16.99**

Practicing the Sacred Art of Listening
A Guide to Enrich Your Relationships and Kindle Your Spiritual Life
By Kay Lindahl 8 x 8, 176 pp, Quality PB, 978-1-893361-85-0 **$18.99**

Recovery—The Sacred Art: The Twelve Steps as Spiritual Practice *By Rami Shapiro*
Foreword by Joan Borysenko, PhD 5½ x 8½, 240 pp, Quality PB, 978-1-59473-259-1 **$16.99**

Running—The Sacred Art: Preparing to Practice *By Dr. Warren A. Kay*
Foreword by Kristin Armstrong 5½ x 8½, 160 pp, Quality PB, 978-1-59473-227-0 **$16.99**

The Sacred Art of Chant: Preparing to Practice
By Ana Hernández 5½ x 8½, 192 pp, Quality PB, 978-1-59473-036-8 **$16.99**

The Sacred Art of Fasting: Preparing to Practice
By Thomas Ryan, CSP 5½ x 8½, 192 pp, Quality PB, 978-1-59473-078-8 **$15.99**

The Sacred Art of Forgiveness: Forgiving Ourselves and Others through God's Grace
By Marcia Ford 8 x 8, 176 pp, Quality PB, 978-1-59473-175-4 **$18.99**

The Sacred Art of Listening: Forty Reflections for Cultivating a Spiritual Practice
By Kay Lindahl; Illus. by Amy Schnapper 8 x 8, 160 pp, b/w illus., Quality PB, 978-1-893361-44-7 **$16.99**

The Sacred Art of Lovingkindness: Preparing to Practice
By Rabbi Rami Shapiro; Foreword by Marcia Ford 5½ x 8½, 176 pp, Quality PB, 978-1-59473-151-8 **$16.99**

Thanking & Blessing—The Sacred Art: Spiritual Vitality through Gratefulness
By Jay Marshall, PhD; Foreword by Philip Gulley 5½ x 8½, 176 pp, Quality PB, 978-1-59473-231-7 **$16.99**

Writing—The Sacred Art: Beyond the Page to Spiritual Practice
By Rami Shapiro and Aaron Shapiro 5½ x 8½, 192 pp, Quality PB, 978-1-59473-372-7 **$16.99**

Spirituality

The Forgiveness Handbook

Spiritual Wisdom and Practice for the Journey to Freedom, Healing and Peace

Created by the Editors at SkyLight Paths; Introduction by The Rev. Canon Marianne Wells Borg

Offers inspiration, encouragement and spiritual practice from across faith traditions for all who seek hope, wholeness and the freedom that comes from true forgiveness.

6 x 9, 256 pp, Quality PB, 978-1-59473-577-6 **$18.99**

Like a Child

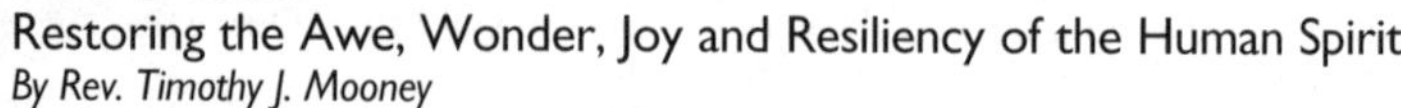

Restoring the Awe, Wonder, Joy and Resiliency of the Human Spirit

By Rev. Timothy J. Mooney

By breaking free from our misperceptions about what it means to be an adult, we can reshape our world and become harbingers of grace. This unique spiritual resource explores Jesus's counsel to become like children in order to enter the kingdom of God. 6 x 9, 160 pp, Quality PB, 978-1-59473-543-1 **$16.99**

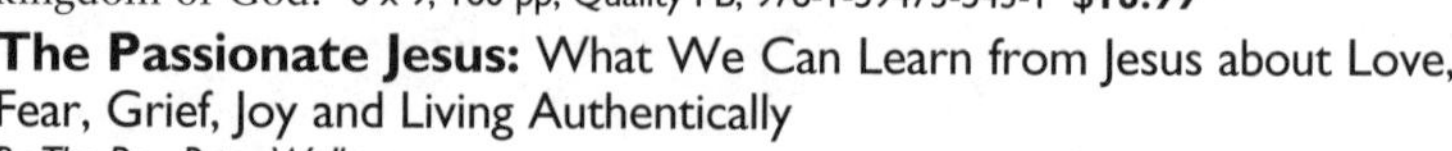

The Passionate Jesus: What We Can Learn from Jesus about Love, Fear, Grief, Joy and Living Authentically

By The Rev. Peter Wallace

Reveals Jesus as a passionate figure who was involved, present, connected, honest and direct with others and encourages you to build personal authenticity in every area of your own life. 6 x 9, 208 pp, Quality PB, 978-1-59473-393-2 **$18.99**

Gathering at God's Table: The Meaning of Mission in the Feast of Faith

By Katharine Jefferts Schori

A profound reminder of our role in the larger frame of God's dream for a restored and reconciled world. 6 x 9, 256 pp, HC, 978-1-59473-316-1 **$21.99**

The Heartbeat of God: Finding the Sacred in the Middle of Everything

By Katharine Jefferts Schori; Foreword by Joan Chittister, OSB

Explores our connections to other people, to other nations and with the environment through the lens of faith.

6 x 9, 240 pp, HC, 978-1-59473-292-8 **$21.99**; Quality PB, 978-1-59473-589-9 **$16.99**

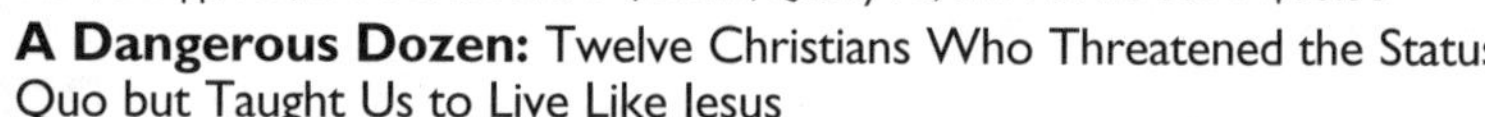

A Dangerous Dozen: Twelve Christians Who Threatened the Status Quo but Taught Us to Live Like Jesus

By The Rev. Canon C. K. Robertson, PhD; Foreword by Archbishop Desmond Tutu

Profiles twelve visionary men and women who challenged society and showed the world a different way of living.

6 x 9, 208 pp, Quality PB, 978-1-59473-298-0 **$16.99**

Laugh Your Way to Grace: Reclaiming the Spiritual Power of Humor

By Rev. Susan Sparks

A powerful, humorous case for laughter as a spiritual, healing path.

6 x 9, 176 pp, Quality PB, 978-1-59473-280-5 **$16.99**

Claiming Earth as Common Ground: The Ecological Crisis through the Lens of Faith
By Andrea Cohen-Kiener; Foreword by Rev. Sally Bingham
6 x 9, 192 pp, Quality PB, 978-1-59473-261-4 **$16.99**

Living into Hope: A Call to Spiritual Action for Such a Time as This
By Rev. Dr. Joan Brown Campbell; Foreword by Karen Armstrong
6 x 9, 208 pp, Quality PB, 978-1-59473-436-6 **$18.99**; HC, 978-1-59473-283-6 **$21.99**

Renewal in the Wilderness
A Spiritual Guide to Connecting with God in the Natural World
By John Lionberger 6 x 9, 176 pp, b/w photos, Quality PB, 978-1-59473-219-5 **$16.99**

Spiritual Adventures in the Snow
Skiing & Snowboarding as Renewal for Your Soul
By Dr. Marcia McFee and Rev. Karen Foster; Foreword by Paul Arthur
5½ x 8½, 208 pp, Quality PB, 978-1-59473-270-6 **$16.99**

A Walk with Four Spiritual Guides: Krishna, Buddha, Jesus, and Ramakrishna
By Andrew Harvey 5½ x 8½, 192 pp, b/w photos & illus., Quality PB, 978-1-59473-138-9 **$15.99**

Spirituality / Animal Companions

Blessing the Animals
Prayers and Ceremonies to Celebrate God's Creatures, Wild and Tame
Edited and with Introductions by Lynn L. Caruso
5 x 7¼, 256 pp, Quality PB, 978-1-59473-253-9 **$15.99**; HC, 978-1-59473-145-7 **$19.99**

Remembering My Pet
A Kid's Own Spiritual Workbook for When a Pet Dies
By Nechama Liss-Levinson, PhD, and Rev. Molly Phinney Baskette, MDiv
Foreword by Lynn L. Caruso
8 x 10, 48 pp, 2-color text, HC, 978-1-59473-221-8 **$16.99**

What Animals Can Teach Us about Spirituality
Inspiring Lessons from Wild and Tame Creatures
By Diana L. Guerrero 6 x 9, 176 pp, Quality PB, 978-1-893361-84-3 **$18.99**

Spirituality & Crafts

Beading—The Creative Spirit
Finding Your Sacred Center through the Art of Beadwork
By Rev. Wendy Ellsworth
Invites you on a spiritual pilgrimage into the kaleidoscope world of glass and color.
7 x 9, 240 pp, 8-page color insert, 40+ b/w photos and 40 diagrams
Quality PB, 978-1-59473-267-6 **$18.99**

Contemplative Crochet
A Hands-On Guide for Interlocking Faith and Craft
By Cindy Crandall-Frazier; Foreword by Linda Skolnik
Illuminates the spiritual lessons you can learn through crocheting.
7 x 9, 208 pp, b/w photos, Quality PB, 978-1-59473-238-6 **$16.99**

The Knitting Way
A Guide to Spiritual Self-Discovery
By Linda Skolnik and Janice MacDaniels
Examines how you can explore and strengthen your spiritual life through knitting.
7 x 9, 240 pp, b/w photos, Quality PB, 978-1-59473-079-5 **$16.99**

The Painting Path
Embodying Spiritual Discovery through Yoga, Brush and Color
By Linda Novick; Foreword by Richard Segalman
Explores the divine connection you can experience through art.
7 x 9, 208 pp, 8-page color insert, plus b/w photos, Quality PB, 978-1-59473-226-3 **$18.99**

The Quilting Path
A Guide to Spiritual Discovery through Fabric, Thread and Kabbalah
By Louise Silk
Explores how to cultivate personal growth through quilt making.
7 x 9, 192 pp, b/w photos and illus., Quality PB, 978-1-59473-206-5 **$16.99**

The Scrapbooking Journey
A Hands-On Guide to Spiritual Discovery
By Cory Richardson-Lauve; Foreword by Stacy Julian
Reveals how this craft can become a practice used to deepen and shape your life.
7 x 9, 176 pp, 8-page color insert, plus b/w photos, Quality PB, 978-1-59473-216-4 **$18.99**

The Soulwork of Clay
A Hands-On Approach to Spirituality
By Marjory Zoet Bankson; Photos by Peter Bankson
Takes you through the seven-step process of making clay into a pot, drawing parallels at each stage to the process of spiritual growth.
7 x 9, 192 pp, b/w photos, Quality PB, 978-1-59473-249-2 **$16.99**

About SKYLIGHT PATHS Publishing

SkyLight Paths Publishing is creating a place where people of different spiritual traditions come together for challenge and inspiration, a place where we can help each other understand the mystery that lies at the heart of our existence.

Through spirituality, our religious beliefs are increasingly becoming a part of our lives—rather than *apart* from our lives. While many of us may be more interested than ever in spiritual growth, we may be less firmly planted in traditional religion. Yet, we do want to deepen our relationship to the sacred, to learn from our own as well as from other faith traditions, and to practice in new ways.

SkyLight Paths sees both believers and seekers as a community that increasingly transcends traditional boundaries of religion and denomination—people wanting to learn from each other, *walking together, finding the way.*

For your information and convenience, at the back of this book we have provided a list of other SkyLight Paths books you might find interesting and useful. They cover the following subjects:

Buddhism / Zen
Catholicism
Children's Books
Christianity
Comparative Religion
Current Events
Earth-Based Spirituality
Enneagram
Global Spiritual Perspectives
Gnosticism
Hinduism / Vedanta
Inspiration
Islam / Sufism
Judaism
Kabbalah
Meditation
Midrash Fiction
Monasticism
Mysticism
Poetry
Prayer
Religious Etiquette
Retirement
Spiritual Biography
Spiritual Direction
Spirituality
Women's Interest
Worship